DESIGN AND STRATEGY
FOR CORPORATE
INFORMATION SERVICES:
MIS Long-Range Planning

DESIGN AND STRATEGY FOR CORPORATE INFORMATION SERVICES:
MIS Long-Range Planning

LARRY E. LONG

Prentice-Hall, Inc.
Englewood Cliffs, New Jersey 07638

Library of Congress Cataloging in Publication Data

Long, Larry E.
  Design and strategy for corporate information services.

  Includes index.
  1. Management information systems. I. Title.
T58.6.L66   658.4'0388   81-13931
ISBN 0-13-201707-5   AACR2

Printed in the United States of America

10 9 8 7 6 5 4 3 2 1

Editorial/production supervision: Nancy Milnamow
Interior design: Nancy Milnamow
Manufacturing buyer: Gordon Osbourne

ISBN 0-13-201707-5

Prentice-Hall International Inc., *London*
Prentice-Hall of Australia Pty. Limited, *Sydney*
Prentice-Hall of Canada, Ltd., *Toronto*
Prentice-Hall of India Private Limited, *New Delhi*
Prentice-Hall of Japan, Inc., *Tokyo*
Prentice-Hall of Southeast Asia Pte. Ltd., *Singapore*
Whitehall Books Limited, Wellington, *New Zealand*

To Pete and Marie

Contents

Preface

Data processing/management information systems (DP/MIS) departments in most companies are the nucleus of corporate operation, though few corporate officers will admit it. The common denominator in any company is the data and information gathered and disseminated throughout the various functional areas. Because of this new-found importance and critical position within the company, DP/MIS (hereafter shortened to MIS) management personnel must make a concentrated effort in strategic planning for corporate information services, an activity often referred to as, simply, MIS long-range planning.

The potential capacity to serve users in most computer centers is much greater than the actual output, even though some computer center directors deny excess capacity and claim saturation. The inefficient operation of many computer centers can be attributed to the lack of MIS long-range planning. Too often, MIS managers, through no fault of their own, are forced to deal primarily with the routine crises of day-to-day activities and planning is given a back seat to getting production work out on time. A comprehensive MIS long-range plan is an integral part of today's successful computer centers; therefore, MIS management personnel who neglect the planning function are doomed to a short-term, crisis-oriented environment.

Unfortunately, the state of the art of strategic MIS long-range planning is well below that of strategic corporate long-range planning and of sister functions throughout the company (marketing, production, accounting, and so on). To make matters worse, expertise is scarce in the area of MIS long-range planning. Integration and productivity have become key words to corporate MIS managers and they are beginning to realize the importance of comprehensive MIS planning. The days are gone when MIS managers could operate by the seat of the pants and handle each situation as it arose. Too much is at stake. The small, one-man shop, as well as the geographically dispersed 4000-man operation, need to address essentially the same facets of MIS long-range planning.

This book presents a methodology for strategic MIS long-range planning that encourages managers and planners to examine and consider all facets of MIS operation. This approach forces managers and planners to think "integration." The end product, an MIS long-range plan, for a given company will probably address only those facets (application systems, education, image, and so on) pertinent to that company.

A common misconception of MIS long-range planning is that it should be oriented to planning for computer hardware and application systems. Certainly these facets of MIS operation are critical to the planning process. However, there exist many peripheral facets that have a significant effect on not only hardware and applications systems planning, but general MIS planning. Almost every corporation can relate to the instance where the lack of MIS planning has resulted in the MIS department and/or the corporation being placed in a predicament that could have been avoided with prior planning. A large department store chain implemented a new point of sale (POS) system and neglected to provide any training for store managers and salespersons on the new system. The result was an enormous loss of sales and untold goodwill. In another case, a computer center found existing machine room space inadequate for new hardware. The new hardware remained in the hallway and implementation of two major systems was delayed for two months while the facilities were expanded. One company's rapidly expanding information services department continued to grow in numbers of employees but occupied the same office space. At the saturation point, space was allocated in another building twenty miles away. The split in personnel and subsequent inefficiencies experienced through lack of project coordination could have been resolved with prior planning.

Many information services departments are handicapped in their abilities to interface with users because information services has long been the corporate "whipping boy" and has suffered image problems. Careful attention to image improvement during the planning process can reverse the corporate attitudes towards MIS and create a more productive environment.

The objective of this book is to provide the reader with a methodology that details the mechanics for developing a comprehensive MIS long-range plan. The orientation is "what" to include and/or consider, not the specifics of "how" to approach a solution to a specific problem. The MIS long-range plan and the accompanying ideas must be sold to users, top management and computer center personnel. This book should provide helpful support justification for selling the plan and the ideas.

Throughout the book all organizational references are to the "corporation," "corporate entities," "corporate managers," and so on. The reference to the corporate environment is simply for clarity and consistency. The MIS long-range (or strategic) planning process described in this book is equally applicable to state, local and federal government agencies, educational institutions and non-profit agencies.

The term data processing (DP) denotes transaction handling. Most computer center operations have transcended DP and now provide management information to aid in decision making. However, the term DP still has tremendous momentum and is used by many corporations. The term management information systems (MIS) is used in this book to denote the expanded function of DP; however, DP and MIS are interchangeable in the context of this book. For variety, the corporate entity that performs the MIS function is referenced as the computer center, MIS department and (corporate) information services.

Occasional references will be made to small, medium and large MIS departments. Throughout this book, an arbitrary assumption is made that the total number of MIS professionals determines the size. Small, medium and large departments are 25 or less, 26-175 and 176 and more, respectively. Although the scope and depth of detail of the planning process may vary between large and small MIS departments, the MIS long-range planning methodology presented in this book is equally applicable to each. Similarly, the methodology accommodates planning for centralized facilities and for DDP (distributed data processing) environments.

It is recommended that someone wishing to use this book as a guide to MIS long-range planning read straight through the book to get a feeling for the scope of a comprehensive MIS long-range plan. This initial reading will provide the planner with a better perspective on MIS long-range planning. During this reading the planner should make note of those areas for which planning is appropriate for their organization.

This book would be helpful in varying degrees to anyone directly or indirectly associated with the MIS long-range planning process. Those persons in the following job functions will find this book beneficial:

MIS long-range planner
Director of information services
Managers in MIS operational areas
User managers
Corporate planners
Corporate officers
Members of the high-level MIS steering committee.

The material in this book is presented with the assumption that the reader has a substantial knowledge of the MIS environment. Continuity and brevity are achieved, since the written material can close quickly to the point and items can simply be listed without further explanation.

Design and Strategy for Corporate Information Services is divided into three parts:

Part I: Overview
Part II: Methodology
Part III: Planning Areas.

After the reader has gained a general knowledge of MIS long-range planning from the material presented in Chapter 1 and heeded the warnings of Chapter 2, the planner is ready to commence the MIS long-range planning process. Part II presents a three-phased MIS long-range planning methodology that is graphically illustrated in Chapter 3. The three phases of preparation, development, and implementation and maintenance are discussed in detail in Chapters 4, 5 and 6, respectively. Part III, Planning Areas, presents detailed discussions of strategies, approaches and considerations in each of the major MIS planning areas.

Scores of MIS professionals have related to me their MIS planning experiences with the frankness and candor we have come to expect of our colleagues. I would like to thank these contributors, for without their input this book would not have been possible. I would like to also extend my deepest appreciation to Mrs. Elsie W. Hamel for the preparation of the manuscript and to my wife, Dr. Nancy K. Long, for assisting in virtually every phase of the preparation of this book.

Larry E. Long

DESIGN AND STRATEGY
FOR CORPORATE
INFORMATION SERVICES:
MIS Long-Range Planning

Part I

Overview

Chapter 1

The MIS Long-Range Plan:

Introduction

WHAT CAN BE ACCOMPLISHED

The implementation of an MIS long-range plan will create an environment in which MIS can realize a better relationship with users and top management personnel. Systems that are not responsive result in ill feelings. Such ill feelings are irritated by ad hoc selection of internal priorities for application systems development and enhancements. A plan can provide for increasing responsiveness to users via a coordinated plan to integrate functionally adjacent application areas. Also, a strategic MIS plan will instill cooperation among users and top management personnel by encouraging their active participation in the planning process. Continuous feedback from all levels of personnel and all functional areas is a prerequisite to successful MIS planning.

The long-range plan will provide a more efficient allocation of precious corporate resources. By integrating systems and minimizing the need for system changes over a multiyear period, MIS management will be better able to schedule their limited resources over a longer time horizon. This efficient mode of long-term scheduling will free resources and allow for an expanded scope of MIS services. Too often the corporate information services function becomes involved voluntarily or involuntarily in activities that waste resources and do not contribute to corporate or MIS goals. When resources are judiciously allocated well in advance and reasonable priorities are established for MIS projects, MIS is not obligated to respond to the whims of user managers. Even though many requests for service from user managers are justified, many are not well conceived nor are all the ramifications considered. The latter can be eliminated via an MIS long-range plan.

Another aspect of an MIS long-range plan is that it can be used as a benchmark for performance both internal and external to the MIS department. Since the long-range plan identifies projects and milestones, it is a good vehicle for personnel and department performance evaluation.

A good MIS long-range plan should make a significant contribution to corporate profit. This contribution will be made in the form of better utilization of personnel and equipment and through systems that are more responsive to user needs. Such systems have an effect on the balance sheet through reduced inventory, better customer relations, and other factors.

The MIS long-range plan provides the foundation for the coordination of all future MIS activities. Traditionally, corporate application systems have grown as autonomous units because of immediate needs. Management information systems now and in the future should be integrated. Virtually all facets of corporate operation are linked by data and information passing through the computing center. Any company not undertaking an MIS long-range plan is forgoing a valuable opportunity to coordinate future application systems activities.

A long-range plan has another notable benefit to the corporation. The planning process forces management to think abstractly. Too often managers are restricted (by time) to responding to routine activities. The MIS long-range plan forces managers and planners to take a hard look at information processing. The results of abstract thinking are ideas and a better understanding for all.

STATE OF THE ART OF MIS LONG-RANGE PLANNING

MIS planning is probably ten to fifteen years behind the state of the art of corporate planning, perhaps even more. Executive committees of large and small corporations have been developing plans with horizons from three to twenty years since the turn of the century. Only a few years back, most MIS departments were planning little more than one year in advance. Even large-scale MIS projects, which were known to take more than one year, were planned, approved, and developed without a specific timetable for completion.

Many corporations are experiencing rapid growth. The corporate growth in facilities and/or products and/or services is often undetermined one year in advance. These rapid-growth corporations wreak havoc on the MIS long-range planning process and the MIS function in general. Too often, MIS directors are not forewarned of anticipated changes. Corporate managers underestimate the effect that these changes have on the MIS function. The addition of an extra digit to the employee number may require person-years of effort.

Whether in the MIS department or in other functional areas, planning is often viewed as an additional duty and a chore. Is it a chore or an exciting, stimulating responsibility; or is it somewhere in between? Planning becomes a chore, in particular, when it is a task that is over and above the regular assigned routine activities and is not considered as a part of the job function. Planning is a management function and should be included as a part of each manager's formal job description.

Of all operational departments within a given corporation, no department operates under more pressure than MIS. Certainly, production has schedules to meet and accounting has end-of-year closing to meet, but in these and other cases they are also very heavily dependent on the output from the information services department. Therefore, pressing deadlines from every corner of the corporate endeavor also become pressing deadlines for information services. Under these circumstances, time becomes a premium to all concerned. All too often, unsympathetic corporate management demands attention to these everyday routine matters, making planning a function that may or may not be accomplished, depending upon the amount of time available. Unfortunately, a visible planning function is the first to be cut in times of limited monetary resources. It is difficult for MIS personnel to develop a high level of expertise in MIS long-range planning in this environment.

MIS long-range planning is a relatively new activity that has evolved in recent years because of a desperate need for corporate coordination of data storage and information dissemination. Like any technical activity, the learning process is slow and several years may elapse before an effective long-range plan can be compiled.

For whatever reasons, most corporate long-range plans deal directly with the corporation's product or service and often do not consider the effects on the MIS function; therefore, the MIS function is usually not considered at the corporate level.

Only a small percentage of the computer centers have effective MIS long-range plans. For those that have plans, the plans are brief, short range, and are usually limited to hardware planning and/or applications software planning. Expect this situation to change in the near future. MIS long-range planning is far too critical to be overlooked much longer.

SCOPE OF THE MIS PLANNING FUNCTION

The MIS long-range plan should include events and activities which are affected by or under the control of the information services (or MIS) department. This includes all facets of MIS which play on effectiveness and efficiency of MIS operation, both internal and external to the corporation. The long-range plan for MIS is more than just goals and objectives or hardware acquisition planning. It encompasses not only the peripheral activities internal to the MIS department, but the long-range systems objectives of the functional departments that are serviced by information.

INTEGRATION THROUGH MIS LONG-RANGE PLANNING

The MIS long-range plan can be used to integrate the functional areas of the company. The typical corporate approach to better integration of corporate entities is to revise the structural organization of the corporation. Some corporations have been radically overhauled at each level of command with no improvement in overall integration. Corporate reorganization can be beneficial, but the real common denominator and the best vehicle by which to integrate corporate operations is information. The MIS long-range plan can be a valuable aid in realizing an effective and efficient flow of information throughout the corporation.

OBJECTIVES OF MIS LONG-RANGE PLANNING

The ultimate objective of MIS long-range planning is to improve the communication link and thereby the level of cooperation among the various levels of corporate management and functionally adjacent operational departments. The MIS long-range plan will provide a vehicle for a coordinated effort that will make MIS planning possible and, as a result, information systems will be more responsive to user needs. The peripheral objectives of the plan are to improve management's potential to provide accurate estimates of resource requirements and, subsequently, an efficient allocation of these resources over both the short and the long term.

The mere execution of the planning process will identify areas that need improvement and identify potential areas for work simplification and cost reduction. Upon examination of various applications, both existing and proposed, a long-range plan will provide insight into those which are good and those which are of marginal value, those which should be either terminated or not considered for future upgrades. A successful MIS long-range plan and the planning process will provide corporate visibility to data processing and provide an environment that will foster cooperation.

REASONS FOR MIS LONG-RANGE PLANNING

The computer-based information systems environment is extremely volatile, especially with respect to technology change. To accommodate this changing technology, managers need to develop contingency plans to be prepared for the rapid changes in state-of-the-art technology. Some people, however, would interpret this statement as justification against planning. Those people would say to wait until the change occurs and make the adjustments based on that which is known. MIS managers of today must gaze periodically into the crystal ball and make intelligent and informed forecasts of future technological developments and subsequently make plans for expected new equipment and software announcements.

The state of the art of hardware and software technology is growing exponentially. The ability of MIS professionals to cope effectively with this technology and thereby realize its benefits is a problem. The rate of growth of management techniques is somewhat less than that of the technology. The ever-widening gap between the technology and the manager's ability to cope with that technology is illustrated in Figure 1-1. It is uniformly recognized by most corporations that, overall, management of the information services function is not realizing its potential. An MIS long-range plan can effectively narrow the gap and allow MIS management personnel to take advantage of the benefits derived from a rapidly changing technology.

For many companies, especially government agencies, the lead time required to purchase new equipment is substantial. The approval process may take from one to five years to complete. In these cases, managers must plan today for the implementation of tomorrow's technology.

Certainly, one of the most visible pressures for MIS long-range planning is the scarcity of professionals in the area of MIS. The scarcity of trained and perceptive

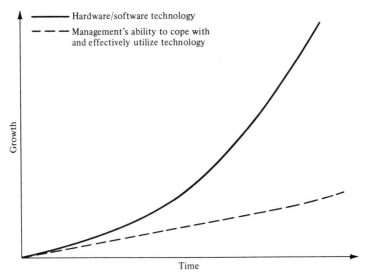

Figure 1-1. *Ever-widening gap between computer tech-nology and management techniques.*

systems analysts and programmers is real. Traditionally, good MIS managers are few and far between. The lead time for training an experienced MIS professional is from one to three years, depending upon the specialty area. Even a well-trained professional is usually not operating at full efficiency until after the first year of employment at a particular company.

In general, there is a scarcity of other company resources, as well. Especially in MIS, the number of projects proposed is usually greater than the amount of available resources required to complete them. The implementation of a management information system is simply one of many strategic investment opportunities in which a company can invest its resources. An MIS should be evaluated in the same manner as a new product line or a new machine tool.

The recent trends toward corporate integration via data and information and distributed processing require coordinated planning for future management information systems. A user must be cognizant that another user in a functionally adjacent application may benefit from expansion of his system at some time in the future. As an example, an upgrade to the payroll system will certainly affect the personnel system, especially if the files are shared between the two application subsystems.

REASONS TO AVOID MIS LONG-RANGE PLANNING

In most corporations, especially those that have had an operational data processing/information services department for fifteen years or more, the frequency and randomness of user demands may negate efforts at MIS long-range planning. Minor changes to existing systems as well as major new systems proposals are continuous inputs into the MIS manager's "in basket."

Even after detailed specifications have been "frozen," systems requirements are often revised and, in many cases, may drastically change the complexion of a project. When this occurs, the original estimates of personnel requirements and dollars are invalidated, but even worse, efforts at work-load leveling and budgeting are invalidated.

The MIS profession is notorious for a high rate of personnel turnover. A project conceived by one person might be completed by another. A high rate of personnel turnover often creates the three-steps-forward, two-steps-backward syndrome. That is, every time an individual is hired, a certain learning process must take place, even with experienced personnel. Very seldom does a new hire take over where his or her predecessor left off.

As indicated earlier in the reasons for long-range planning, many would argue that the fast pace of hardware and software changes is justification for avoiding long-range planning. Why not just wait until the technology is announced and then react? Some MIS departments prefer this more conservative reactive mode of operation.

Another very real argument for avoiding the planning process is that the planning function is a resource drain. Personnel must be diverted from so-called "productive" tasks. However, it should be noted that planning is much like systems documentation. You can get along without it, especially when talking about "now," but as the absence of documentation will haunt you later, so will the absence of an MIS long-range plan.

In the final analysis, if one were to list the advantages and disadvantages of MIS long-range planning side by side for any given corporation, the decision is obvious. An MIS long-range plan is a necessity.

LONG-RANGE PLANNING AND FORECASTING

The relationship between long-range planning and forecasting is that forecasting is part of the long-range plan. The term "forecast" implies an attempt to depict that which will happen in the future. MIS managers must gaze into the crystal ball and forecast certain events: hardware, software, corporate and national economy, future expenditures, receipts for services and many other areas. These forecasts provide valuable input to and are an integral part of the planning process. The long-range plan may address various alternatives and directions that could be taken, depending on the outcome of events.

CORPORATE AND MIS LONG-RANGE PLANNING

Unless the director of MIS is on the executive committee (usually the chairman of the board, president, and senior vice-presidents), topics relating to MIS planning are seldom discussed during executive committee meetings. Corporate plans may include a new product line, new warehouses, increases in personnel, or a new salary and wage structure. All of these topics have a direct effect on MIS, yet typically the MIS topic is avoided.

Why is this the case? Corporate management may still consider DP or MIS as a peripheral function. More often than not, the information services function is relegated to being several levels below the other major functional areas of the corporation even though the MIS budget may be commensurate with other major corporate entities. For example, in only twenty years an MIS department of a medium-sized corporation grew from a two-person operation to that of several hundred people, yet there has been no effort to accommodate this change in the corporate organizational structure. Corporate managers are still insecure about their ability to talk with MIS professionals or about the many facets of management information systems.

It is the responsibility of the MIS long-range planner to seek actively the cooperation of high-level corporate officers. It is the rare company that has organizational entities not supported by, or in most cases, entirely dependent on a successful MIS operation. Unfortunately, MIS is more often taken for granted than appreciated.

The advantages of corporate and MIS cooperation in planning are overwhelming. First, if MIS personnel are made aware of the overall company objectives, they can subsequently develop priorities realistically. Second, MIS long-range planning helps executives to know and understand the goals and targets of MIS. They can develop an awareness and sympathy of the limitations of MIS and the ramifications of certain corporate decisions on the effectiveness of the information services function. Third, and perhaps most important, what is usually a highly developed corporate planning expertise can be transferred to the MIS planning function.

Long-range planning, especially with horizons of three or more years, is still a function of top management personnel. Unfortunately, as the number of levels between the chief executive officer and the director of MIS increases, the ultimate effectiveness of the MIS long-range plan will decrease. This is because of the organizational remoteness of MIS from the ongoing corporate planning process. No matter where MIS is located, the chief executive officer and the executive committee must not only be involved in the MIS long-range planning process, but ultimately approve and thereby make a commitment to those activities identified and described in the MIS long-range plan. An MIS long-range plan, even if mechanically very well done, will mean nothing without top-level approval. The MIS long-range planner should be aware that unless top management is involved and kept abreast of the scope and progress of the MIS long-range plan, the probability of unilateral approval will be much less. Time expended on circulating progress reports and making oral presentations to top management personnel as a group and individually will be well spent.

The question might be raised as to why MIS long-range planning is not included in corporate long-range planning. Certain general facets of MIS planning should be included in the corporate long-range plan; however, an effective MIS long-range plan is a document which requires a level of detail that is not appropriate for a corporate long-range plan. The MIS plan should be an outgrowth of the corporate plan and should include details of implementation of those thrusts, goals, and objectives established in the corporate plan. Planned corporate expansion (extra warehouses, new retail outlets, increases in personnel) should be closely coordinated with MIS. The lead times required for necessary software modifications and hardware upgrades are significant and should be considered. A typical corporate long-range plan has, at a minimum, a ten-year horizon, with fifteen- and twenty-year horizons more common. For decades, corporations have required long-range plans from marketing and production. These subordinate plans provide detailed support to the corporate long-range plan, but the horizon is usually no greater than five years. Information is not only the catalyst but the vehicle for overall corporate integration. It stands to reason that an MIS long-range plan should be commissioned and then supported by the executive committee and the corporate long-range planning function. Like plans for marketing and production, the MIS long-range plan would be in support of the corporate long-range plan and should parallel the major thrusts of the corporation. For example, one department store chain announced the opening of a new store within the next three months, then opened three during that time period. The point-of-sale hardware was completely overloaded. A small manufacturing concern acquired a similar manufacturing firm and centralized MIS in hopes that existing equipment could handle those functions being handled by that firm's data-processing department. Of course, this was not the case.

FACTORS AFFECTING MIS PLANNING

When the planner views the organization from the top to the bottom, it becomes apparent that there are essentially four levels of activity within the corporation. From top to bottom, these levels are: strategic, tactical, operational, and clerical.

Managers at the strategic level are primarily objective minded. Their MIS requirements are often one-time reports and "what if" reports. Typically, strategic planning has a horizon longer than three years.

At the tactical level, managers concentrate on achieving a series of goals required to meet the objectives set at the strategic level. The information requirements are more periodic at this level, but managers still require "what if" reports. The horizon at the tactical level is typically from one to three years. These managers are concerned primarily with operations and budgets from year to year.

Personnel at the operational level have well-defined tasks that might span a day, a week, or as much as three months, but their tasks are essentially short term. Their information requirements are performance reports and reports required for immediate operational feedback. The planning horizon at the operational level is seldom greater than one year.

Clerical-level personnel are concerned primarily with the transaction-handling portion of an MIS. The process is repetitive and has a short-range outlook. Planning for clerical-level tasks would have an extremely short horizon. Clerical is used in the generic sense to refer to persons involved in repetitive tasks.

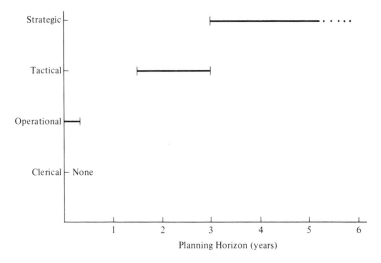

Figure 1-2. *Possible planning horizons at various levels of activity.*

Upon examining the information requirements at the various levels of activities, it is apparent that time horizons and level of detail for project planning must be adjusted relative to the various levels of activity. See Figure 1-2 for a graphic illustration of the planning horizons at the various levels of activity.

The planner may be responsible for describing and/or conceptualizing future corporate MISs. To obtain sufficient knowledge of requirements and scope of a particular MIS project, the planner should touch base with personnel at each level of activity in order to get the proper perspective on an MIS project, because each level perceives an MIS differently.

MIS GROWTH PATTERN

Computer centers, like human beings, have a rather standard pattern of growth during the first five to twenty years, depending upon the sophistication of the computer center. Some human beings mature earlier than others, and so it is with computer centers. Growth patterns after a computer center has reached a state of controlled growth are far less predictable. However, during the initial period of growth, certain events can be predicted with a reasonable amount of success. A typical growth pattern is shown in Figure 1-3.

After implementation of an initial computer, traditional applications with fast paybacks become operational and the organization usually experiences some success with data processing. As the success stories spread throughout the organization, more and more users search for ways in which the computer can be used to serve their

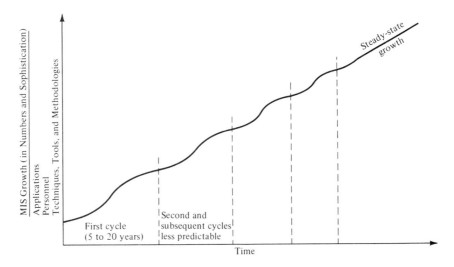

Figure 1-3. *MIS long-term growth pattern.*

needs. The computer center then experiences a rapid growth for one to ten years. This rapid growth usually takes place in the absence of standardized procedures and documentation practices. Systems developed during this era are usually less than the user expected, primarily as a result of a lack of standards, high-level cooperation, and a crisis-oriented operation. Sooner or later, management recognizes that this uncontrolled expansion must cease. A slow-down in new systems development is initiated and efforts are made to clean up existing systems and set standards for future systems. This period in the growth pattern may last from one to four years. Growth after standardized procedures and methodologies have been established is much less predictable, but for organizations still experiencing growing pains, the planner can use this growth pattern as a road map.

This growth can be in application systems, in sophistication of personnel and organization, in management techniques, and in other areas of MIS endeavor. The important thing to realize for the long-range planner is that the identification of the corporate position on the growth pattern may provide insight into what might be expected to occur in the future. For example, if you feel that within the next year or so a slow-down in new systems development will be implemented, then the array of projects might be oriented to development of methodologies and procedures manuals, reorganization, updating system documentation, and so on, and the implementation of these new methods, procedures, and organization.

After a computer center has completed the initial cycle of the growth pattern, the cycle repeats itself with rapid growth, followed by a cleanup period. These cycles can be expected to repeat themselves with ever-increasing frequency until ultimate MIS growth is smooth and totally under control. Some corporations have entered the second cycle with the introduction of DDP (distributed data processing). At the time of this writing, none are even close to entering the third cycle. Realistically, a major technological innovation is necessary to make the third cycle possible. As illustrated in Figure 1-3, a controlled steady-state growth of the information services function will not be realized until a corporation has passed through several cycles. Certainly, no MIS department enjoys such a steady-state growth at this writing.*

SUMMARY

An MIS long-range plan coordinates the activities of the entire company through information processing and information flow. The planning process encourages the company to consider integration of functionally adjacent activities, thereby making the entire operation of the corporation more efficient and effective.

Although a challenging, time-consuming, and politically difficult task, a comprehensive MIS long-range plan will pay for itself many times over.

---

* Definitive descriptions of the various "stages" of MIS growth can be found in Cyrus F. Gibson and Richard L. Nolan's classic treatise, "Managing the Four Stages of EDP Growth," *Harvard Business Review*, January-February 1974. Nolan's followup article "Managing the Crisis in Data Processing," *Harvard Business Review*, March-April 1974, also provides insight into the patterns of MIS growth.

Chapter 2

Warnings

If the long-range planner has an awareness of potential pitfalls before commencing the long-range planning process, he or she may take precautions to avoid making the same mistakes that others have made. This chapter recounts the errors of others in hopes these pitfalls can be avoided in future plans.

AVOID AD HOC PLANNING

Too often the decision to begin an MIS long-range plan is made on an ad hoc basis and, consequently, the assignment is accomplished on an ad hoc basis. The development of a long-range plan is a major project within itself and requires extensive planning before the first interview is made or the first word is written. The planner should have a clear understanding of the procedure that he or she wishes to follow from start to finish. In short, the planner must have a plan for the planning process. Adherence to the methodology presented in this book precludes the possibility of a haphazard planning.

ENSURE RECOGNITION OF THE NEED FOR MIS PLANNING

One of the obvious pitfalls is that MIS management does not recognize the need for MIS long-range planning. In these cases, efforts to develop a plan are approached half-heartedly and not given the attention necessary to produce an effective end product. To overcome the recognition dilemma, the planner should give formal and informal group and individual presentations, and/or distribute written statements to give the MIS plan visibility and to promote understanding.

RECOGNIZE THE 80/20 RULE

User and MIS personnel often get carried away with the potential of a computer-based information system for a particular application area. Each should be aware that the 80/20 rule is applicable; that is, 80% of the necessary data and information can be obtained with only 20% of the effort required to realize the full potential of the information system. An information system has degrees of sophistication. Today, limited resources preclude the luxury of channeling all resources to a few select development projects. Assuming that the 80/20 rule is applicable, the implementation of a system at the highest level of sophistication would require five times the effort of simply attending to the critical 80%.

Rather than attack a few application areas with great intensity, perhaps a better planning strategy would be to get all critical systems operational, then attend to higher levels of sophistication as the availability of time and resources permits.

INVOLVE THOSE PERSONS AFFECTED BY THE PLAN

The MIS long-range plan cannot be accomplished in isolation, especially in isolation from user personnel. The plan is a cooperative effort between functional areas and the various operational units of the MIS department. One person, a team of persons, or a committee may be designated as the functionaries, but planning is an iterative process and requires continuous feedback from those entities and persons who are affected by the plan. A plan accomplished in isolation is an exercise in futility, for no one will accept the end product. Ongoing involvement of all concerned is critical.

BE CONSERVATIVE IN SCOPE

Do not undertake the development of an MIS long-range plan beyond the scope or resources of the organization. A plan that schedules projects which extend personnel and dollar resources to their limit can backfire and cause more harm than good. If anything, the MIS long-range plan should reflect a conservative posture. Remember, the plan is a commitment to accomplish certain tasks by given times. Over-commitments now may placate user expectations on the short term, but do irreparable damage to the integrity of information processing over the long term.

MIS PLANNING IS THE RESPONSIBILITY OF MIS MANAGEMENT

Planning is a management function and it is the responsibility of management to address the issues and to set objectives and strategy over the long term. Although the mechanics of the MIS long-range planning process can be accomplished by senior staff personnel, the responsibility still resides with MIS management. A mistake that some managers have made is to delegate the MIS long-range planning function to computer center staff and/or managers and then ask to be advised when the plan is complete. MIS managers sometimes avoid this responsibility by retaining consultants to accomplish the long-range plan. This is not only an expensive proposition, but unnecessary, and in many cases counterproductive. A good consultant can be helpful in getting started and can provide guidance and direction in the planning process, but the immediate staff should carry out the actual planning function. MIS planning expertise is rare and once developed, should be retained in the company.

PLANNING SHOULD BE PART OF THE DAILY ROUTINE

MIS planning should not be considered a luxury but part of the routine activities of the corporation. As is the case in so many environments, not only MIS, management becomes engrossed in current and routine problems of the day and, consequently, spends insufficient time on long-range planning. Ironically, a long-range plan, when implemented, allows managers to spend more time on major problems and to delegate more authority to subordinates to solve routine problems. This is possible because of the a priori knowledge of activities provided by the MIS long-range plan.

EMPHASIZE SERVICE, NOT HARDWARE

Too often there is an overemphasis on implementation of the latest technology. This overemphasis causes planners to overlook the fundamental need of providing cost-effective service to the users. That "more and better computer capabilities will solve the problem" is a myth. The constant planning for implementation of state-of-the-art technology will only compound existing internal problems. Hardware planning is only a small part of the total planning process.

THE RESULTANT PLAN SHOULD BE EASILY UNDERSTOOD

Portions of the long-range plan should be broad. Goals and objectives can be stated in general terms. This does not mean that the long-range plan should be vague. Goals and objectives should be presented in a format that is not subject to a variety of interpretations. Any section of the plan that cannot be clearly understood by the reader will be misinterpreted or neglected.

USE THE MIS PLAN FOR PERFORMANCE EVALUATION

The MIS long-range plan is a vehicle by which to measure overall MIS performance, especially managerial performance. A common problem is to develop a comprehensive long-range plan and not provide the necessary incentive to achieve the goals set by it. The long-range plan gives management an opportunity to provide input to the planning process and render approval to the plan. The plan is a contract for which individuals should be held accountable. It will gather dust if they are not held accountable for meeting objectives set forth in the long-range plan.

RECOGNIZE POLITICAL REALITIES

The planning process requires the planner to identify shortcomings in a variety of areas. The planner does not set out to be critical of individuals; however, a manager cannot help but take personally those comments that identify shortcomings in an area under his or her control. Inevitably, the planner will step on toes, but this can be done graciously. At the onset of the process many people will be reluctant to cooperate. Do not alienate those people! No key individual can be omitted from the planning process just because of a personality conflict.

SELL THE MIS PLANNING CONCEPT

Corporate officers are only now beginning to recognize the direct relationship between MIS planning and MIS effectiveness. This recognition is a requirement for success. For those corporations whose top management is still uncomfortable with MIS long-range planning, an MIS long-range plan still must be methodically justified and sold to top management. In these cases, a plan that is not "pre-sold" will not be approved.

Part II

Methodology

Chapter 3

The MIS Long-Range
Planning Methodology

Part II of this book presents an MIS long-range planning methodology that is supported in theory and concept in Part I, and with recommendations, considerations, approaches, and strategies in Part III. A three-phase MIS long-range planning methodology is illustrated via work flow diagrams in Figures 3-1, 3-2, and 3-3. Ingredients essential to the MIS planning process are presented in this methodology. The methodology presented in this book is equally appropriate for industry, government, and education, for large and small MIS functions, and for centralized and distributed environments.

Unless a certain amount of rigor is associated with the planning process, corporate, user, and MIS personnel have a tendency to take shortcuts. The existence of a methodology ensures that duties and responsibilities are well defined and that those concerned are involved and have not only continuous input, but some veto power on those aspects of the plan that affect their destiny. Having a methodology also ensures that no area which affects the MIS function is overlooked.

Many corporations have introduced some level of rigor into the MIS planning process—from a simple checklist to a comprehensive methodology. If the company has the beginnings of a planning methodology, the contents of this book can be used to supply the details necessary to complete it. Those companies having a comprehensive methodology can use the contents of this book to complement their existing methodology. Companies with no foundation for MIS planning can use the methodology intact or in a modified form. The methodology presented in Part II is fundamental and can be easily modified to accommodate a given environment. Parts I and III, although supportive of Part II, are equally supportive of any other methodology that encompasses the primary ingredients of the MIS planning process.

There is no magic approach to MIS long-range planning which, if followed, would ensure that all pieces automatically fall into place. The MIS planning function encompasses virtually every functional area within the corporation and requires not

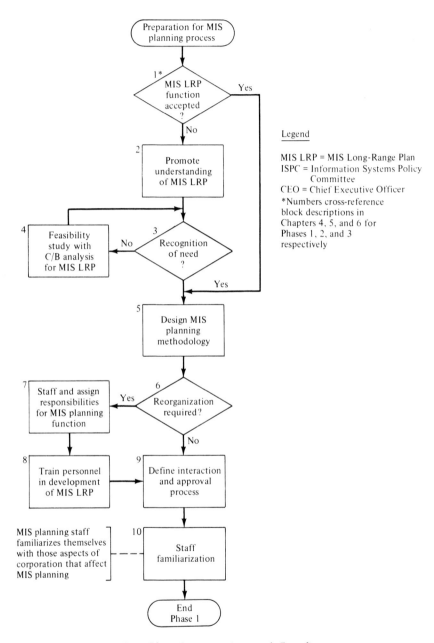

Figure 3-1. *Phase 1: preparation, work flow diagram.*

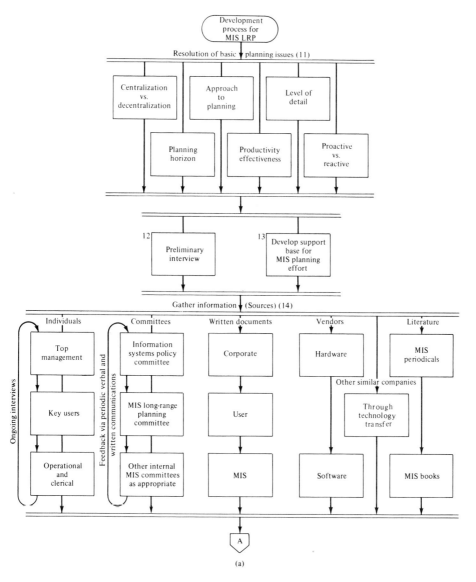

Figure 3-2. Phase 2: development process, work flow diagram.

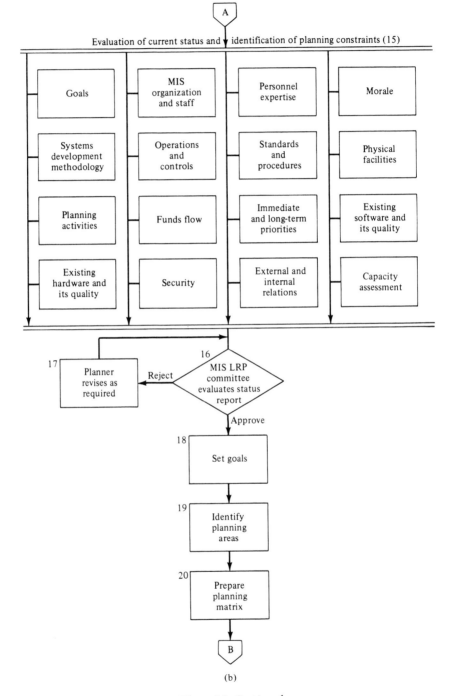

Figure 3.2 Continued

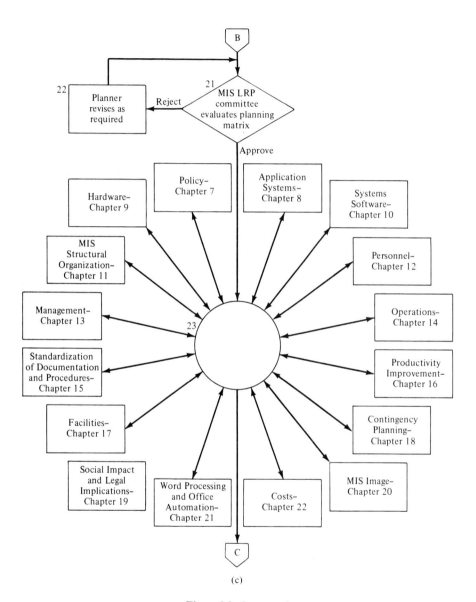

Figure 3.2 *Continued*

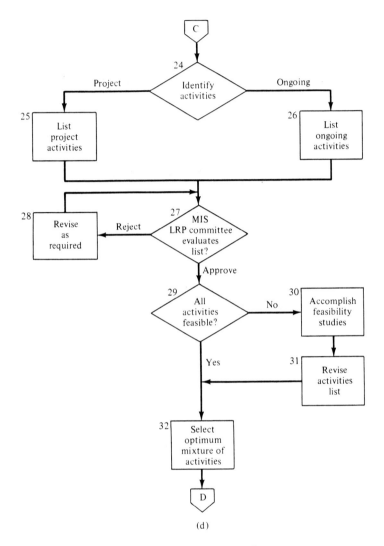

(d)

Figure 3.2 Continued

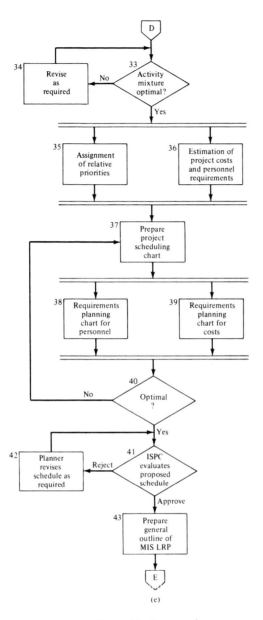

Figure 3.2 *Continued*

27

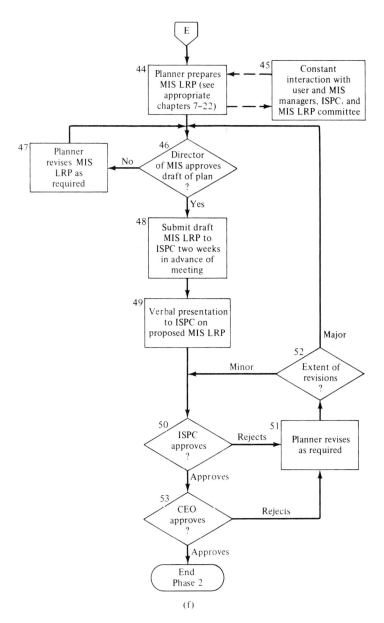

Figure 3.2 Continued

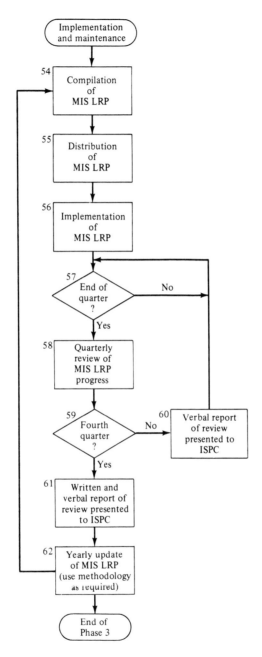

Figure 3-3. Phase 3: implementation and maintenance, work flow diagram.

only the cooperation of representatives of these areas, but their coordination. Adherence to a rigorous planning methodology is the best vehicle to affect this cooperation and coordination.

MIS LONG-RANGE PLANNING WORK FLOW DIAGRAM

The work flow diagrams presented in Figures 3-1, 3-2, and 3-3 illustrate the sequence of major activities and interactions of the MIS long-range planner during the MIS planning process. For continuity, the work flow diagrams of all three phases are presented in this chapter. Since users and other non-MIS personnel will use the work flow diagrams for references, a minimum set of basic flowchart symbols are used to facilitate ease of understanding. The two main symbols used are the process (rectangle) and decision (diamond). The other symbols are terminal (oval) and off-page connector (pentagon). Each of the process and decision symbols is referred to as a block and represents an activity. Each block has an associated number placed outside the upper left corner. These numbers do not necessarily depict the order of execution of the activities. They serve as a cross-reference to more detailed block descriptions in Chapters 4, 5, and 6. The block descriptions provide space to elaborate on such items as personnel involved, responsibilities, criteria for decisions, considerations, approaches to a solution, and where to look for information.

Chapter 4

Phase 1: Preparation

Before the planner can effectively begin the MIS long-range planning process, certain preparations must be made. These preparations involve attitudes, design, organization, education, and familiarization. The neglect of any of these preliminary considerations could make the development of an MIS long-range plan unnecessarily difficult.

The block descriptions for Phase 1, Preparation, are presented in this chapter. The numbered block descriptions cross-reference the activities depicted in the work flow diagram, Figure 3-1.

BLOCK DESCRIPTIONS—PHASE 1

1. The planner and director of information services (MIS) assess whether or not managers, both MIS and corporate, understand and accept the MIS long-range planning function as critical to meeting corporate objectives. Inevitably, an MIS long-range planning project will require a significant commitment of personnel throughout the company. If corporate officials and other MIS managers do not comprehend the scope of the MIS planning function, it is encumbent upon the planner to provide the information necessary to raise their MIS long-range planning awareness. Less than complete acceptance of the merits of MIS long-range planning will result in less than the needed full cooperation.

A prerequisite to a successful corporate information services function is a comprehensive MIS long-range plan. However, there are two prerequisites to developing and implementing such a plan. These are:

A. A knowledge and awareness of computers and information systems on the part of user managers and corporate officers.
B. A realistic assessment and recognition by user managers and corporate officers of the very significant role played by the MIS department.

The latter requires not only a passive recognition but an active emphasis on information services and MIS. Unfortunately, this recognition is often achieved after the occurrence of a catastrophic event that affects the computer center and brings corporate operations to a standstill. A far superior proactive approach to achieving recognition is to implement an ongoing user MIS education program.

Implementation of the latest development techniques, managerial innovations, and the comprehensive MIS long-range plan is, at best, an uphill battle, if functional area managers and corporate officers do not afford the MIS department its proper place and emphasis in corporate operations. An ongoing in-house user education program is the most effective method by which to foster this recognition. User awareness and knowledge of the scope and effect of MIS operations is usually sufficient and makes comprehensive MIS long-range planning and subsequent plan implementation possible. See Chapter 12 for a discussion of in-house user education programs.

2. The planner and/or director of MIS can help managers recognize the need for the MIS planning function by meeting with them individually and in groups to explain what can be accomplished with MIS planning (see Chapter 1). Over the long term, the planner should work toward the implementation of an ongoing in-house user management education program.

3. If formal presentations and personal interactions are not sufficient to convince managers of the worth of MIS long-range planning, the only alternative is to prepare a written report that illustrates the overwhelming benefits derived from MIS long-range planning.

4. A fact of business interaction is that verbal presentations are far more convincing when accompanied by formal written documents. For some, the benefits of MIS planning, such as system integration, need to be documented before managers will accept them. A feasibility study that weighs the cost (personnel requirements and dollars) against the tangible and intangible benefits (see Chapter 1) can be very convincing.

In most cases the feasibility study will be unnecessary. In those instances where it is necessary, the funds and time spent to ensure complete cooperation are easily justified.

5. An MIS long-range planning methodology is presented in Part II. Whether the planner elects to use an existing methodology, to use the one presented in this book, to modify the one presented in this book, or to create his own, the planner should have some type of planning methodology on which to base the development of the MIS long-range plan (see Chapter 3 for additional comments).

6. A corporation must have the organizational structure and personnel to support the MIS long-range planning function. If one or both do not exist, the

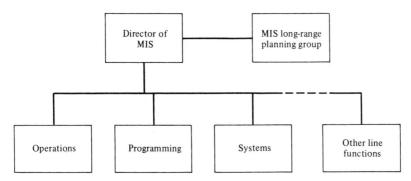

Figure 4-1. Organizational location of the MIS long-range
planner or planning group.

director of MIS must accommodate by designating planning personnel and making
the necessary organizational changes.

    7. The manner in which the planning function is staffed depends on the size of
the organization. In smaller computing centers (professional staff of fewer than
twenty-five persons), MIS managers accomplish the planning function as part of
their routine responsibilities. Even though such a position can be economically
justified, computer centers of this size have difficulty in convincing the personnel
department that a planning position should be established. Computer centers with a
professional staff of more than twenty-five people can easily justify a full-time
coordinator of MIS long-range planning. Since the planner's duties are an extension
of the director's responsibilities, the planner should report to the director of MIS.
This position or group should be a staff (versus line) function to foster a free exchange
of ideas with management (see Figure 4-1). Large computing centers having more
than 175 professionals can justify a small planning group, headed by a senior analyst
or former operational manager, and assisted by two or three others who are familiar
with the corporate MIS environment.
    The terminology used in this book is, for the most part, commonly accepted and
used by MIS professionals. However, certain position titles and groups of persons
are standardized for use in the planning methodology. The positions and groups are
described below in the context of the methodology.

>   *Director of MIS:* the individual charged with the responsibility for all corporate
>   MIS functions (same as director of corporate information services).
>   *MIS Long-Range Planner:* Depending on the size of the company, the director
>   of MIS and the MIS long-range planner may be the same person. Medium
>   and large information services departments usually have a functionary
>   charged with the responsibility for corporate MIS long-range planning.
>   Subsequent references to "planner" refer to the MIS long-range planner.

> *MIS Managers:* managers of the various operational areas within the MIS department (i.e., systems, programming, operations, etc.).
>
> *MIS Long-Range Planning Committee:* a standing committee of operational MIS managers formed to provide continuous input to the MIS long-range planning function.
>
> *Chief Executive Officer:* the operational head of the corporation.
>
> *Executive Committee:* typically, a committee of corporate vice-presidents chaired by the chief executive officer.
>
> *Corporate Officers:* the members of the executive committee plus those charged with responsibilities that span the scope of corporate operations.
>
> *User:* someone who uses the services provided by the MIS department.
>
> *User Manager:* the manager of a functional department and/or division (usually, a budget center) that uses the services provided by the MIS department.
>
> *Information Systems Policy Committee (ISPC):* an arbitrary name given to the high-level MIS steering committee (see Chapter 7 for a detailed description).

The positions and committees defined above support the planning methodology of this book. The director of MIS would need to make the necessary changes in organizational structure and assignments to properly staff the MIS long-range planning function. The MIS long-range planner (in medium-sized and large corporations), the MIS long-range planning committee, and the high-level MIS steering committee are essential to successful MIS planning.

There is no single correct way to organize and staff for the planning function. The prevailing political situation may cause two very similar corporations to select entirely different organizational structures to support MIS planning. The case studies in the Appendix may provide some insight into alternative approaches.

8. As in any technically demanding task, education is a necessity. Those persons assigned MIS long-range planning duties should endeavor to seek education in general planning and MIS planning. The planner would work with the corporation's education coordinator to develop an MIS long-range planning education program. Unfortunately, formal materials for such an education program are limited. Occasionally, professional seminars on MIS long-range planning are offered. The planner should cooperate with the education coordinator to develop a bibliography of books, articles, and periodicals that can be used and updated by future planners.

Because of the paucity of educational materials, perhaps the most effective approach to MIS planning education is through personal interaction with those persons in other companies who have experience in MIS long-range planning. The interaction should focus on the methodology used and the problems encountered.

9. MIS planning is an iterative process that requires a formal, ongoing feedback mechanism and well-defined authority for approval, both intermediate and final. Although MIS and corporate organizational structures have well-defined line author-

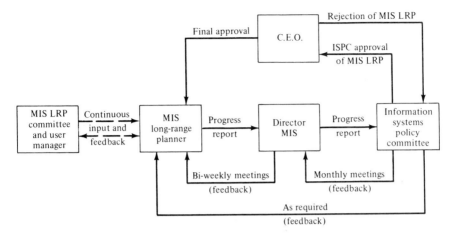

Figure 4-2. *Interaction between principals in the MIS long-range planning process.*

ities, approval authorities for MIS planning are often vague. A formal approval process should be defined by the high-level MIS steering committee (ISPC) and the planner should ensure that all persons involved have a clear understanding of the approval process.

One approach to formalizing the feedback and approval authority process is shown in Figure 4-2. This figure illustrates the ongoing interaction between the principal individuals and committees (chief executive officer, information systems policy committee, director of MIS, MIS long-range planner, MIS long-range planning committee, and user managers).

Initial input and ongoing feedback are provided by the MIS long-range planning committee and operational-level user managers. Feedback is a by-product of the approval procedure for the director of MIS and the ISPC. The planner has biweekly meetings with the director of MIS. The purpose of these meetings is twofold: to obtain direction and guidance from the director, and to make project status reports. The director of MIS interacts with the Information Systems Policy Committee (ISPC) for the same purposes. The communication link from the planner to the ISPC is via the director of MIS. The ISPC has the flexibility to interact directly with the director of MIS or the planner; however, the ISPC has an obligation to communicate the topic of any interaction with the director to the planner. The planner should be privy to all discussions involving MIS planning.

Once the planner has completed the draft of the MIS long-range plan and has the commitments of key personnel throughout the corporation, the plan is submitted to the director of MIS, who can either approve it or recommend that certain revisions be made. Once the director approves the plan, it is routed to the ISPC for approval.

The MIS long-range plan has the potential to affect corporate operation significantly. The ultimate approval of the plan is made at the highest level (ISPC with the blessing of the chief executive officer) to ensure a commitment to implementation.

A rejection at any level sends the plan down the approval chain to the planner for revision. After revising the plan, the planner reinitiates the process by submitting the revised plan to the director.

10. The MIS long-range planning staff, whether a part-time management, individual, or group function, should examine corporate and divisional plans as well as other aspects of corporate operation with which they are not familiar. This might include the product line, organizational structure, various functional areas, geography of facilities, and so on. Most corporations will have a number of descriptive documents that can be helpful. Do not discard a document as not being appropriate because it was printed two years ago. Even if these documents do not reflect the present situation, they may add insight and/or be the only written material on the subject. Printed material can be in the form of manuals, policy statements, directives, memorandums, annual reports, and even training manuals. The planner should have a fundamental knowledge of corporate operational procedures, guidelines, policies, or directives which place constraints on the planning process.

Chapter 5

Phase 2: The Development Process

The activities in Phase 2, the MIS Long-Range Planning Process (Figure 3-2), are described in this chapter. A common mistake made by managers and planners is to omit Phase 1, Preparation for MIS Long-Range Planning, and begin with Phase 2. The outputs of Phase 1—management acceptance, a well-defined planning methodology, and an educated MIS planning staff—are necessary ingredients for successful MIS planning. The following block descriptions assume completion of Phase 1.

BLOCK DESCRIPTIONS—PHASE 2

11. Prior to the commencement of the MIS long-range planning process, certain planning issues should be resolved, considered, or at least identified as having some effect on the planning process.

Planning—Centralized or Decentralized?

In many computing organizations, the centralization/decentralization question is not a problem since virtually all activities are and will remain centralized. However, a growing emphasis on distributed data processing and the extension of the operational aspects of MIS to the user have promoted decentralized thinking. For these companies, certain aspects of planning can be accomplished at the remote site. When one speaks of decentralized planning, he or she also speaks of having more than one person involved in the development of the long-range plan. Even in decentralized planning, however, the planning function must be coordinated at a central site or facility.

The long-range planning function in computer centers of medium to large size is a full-time job for at least one person. When the function is decentralized, remote planners will usually do planning as a secondary function. The primary advantage of decentralized planning is that planners are in a position to be more familiar with specific aspects of the local MIS operation. The disadvantages are that part-time planners sometimes give routine activities higher priority than that of planning activities. It is difficult for remote planners to acquire a global view of the needs and requirements of the total organization. The most apparent advantages of a centralized approach are that a planner is in a position to obtain a global view and that all facets of the plan can be integrated more easily.

Approach to Planning: Top-Down or Bottom-Up?

Both the top-down and bottom-up approaches are appropriate in all organizations and both have advantages. The long-range planning process is most effective when the planner takes advantage of both top-down and bottom-up information gathering.

In top-down planning, the planner can achieve perspective on overall corporate goals, objectives, and trends. Top management may talk in terms of that which is ideal. The lack of top management's cooperation and knowledge of MIS details could preclude the sole use of the top-down approach.

The bottom-up approach places the planner in a position to gather information at the clerical and operational levels of the organization. From this vantage point the planner can get a better perspective of the "real environment." The planner is in a position to note areas of desperate need and to note systems that have marginal benefits to the company.

A combination of the two approaches is a feasible alternative. In effect, the planner is considering the ideal, which was presented at the tactical and strategical levels, and tempering that ideal with the reality of everyday activities at the operational and clerical levels. The actual MIS long-range plan and its proposed activities should reflect a compromise.

Level of Detail

The fact that there exist MIS long-range plans from three pages to five hundred pages in length implies that the level of detail incorporated into an MIS long-range plan can vary widely. It can run from broad statements on MIS goals to wall-clock time estimates of computer runs for particular application systems. The successful MIS long-range plan is, of course, somewhere in between these extremes.

The planner should avoid broad and general policy statements which are subject to interpretation. In cases where such statements are deemed necessary, each should be clarified with supporting statements. The planner should be aware that the physical length of the plan is indirectly proportional to the ultimate level of acceptance and utilization. It is human nature to avoid reading thick, internal corporate documents. If the planner elects to prepare an MIS long-range plan that is extremely detailed, he or she should consider the use of appendices that can be placed in separate volumes.

Whatever the planner's decision, the level of detail should be consistent throughout the plan. That is, the long-range plan should not have fifty pages on hardware planning, four pages on systems planning, and two pages on goals and objectives. Critical elements of MIS operation should be presented such that each topic is covered thoroughly, but concisely.

Planning Horizon

The long-range planner must determine the minimum and maximum planning horizons for the MIS long-range plan. As a rule of thumb, the minimum horizon would be no less than one year. The maximum time horizon covered in the MIS long-range plan can be from three to ten years. Each organization should discuss and decide what they feel to be the optimum horizon for the MIS long-range plan. There is no typical horizon, but an average might be three to five years.

One approach to dealing with increasing uncertainty over time is to provide a long-range plan that has greater detail in years one and two and less detail in years three, four, and five. To accommodate the consistency in level of detail, some corporations have elected multiple long-range plans; for example, a two-year, a five-year, and a ten-year plan. Certainly, this approach is an alternative; however, in practice, three plans can be confusing to use and difficult to maintain.

The long-range planner should give consideration to the time horizon established in the corporate long-range plan. Corporate long-range plans usually deal in greater generality and, therefore, are able to accommodate a greater time horizon (ten or more years). Considering the level of detail necessary for MIS long-range planning and the rapid change in technology, a time horizon of ten years in MIS planning is almost impossible; therefore, coordination of the horizons of the two plans is not an absolute requirement.

Percent of Employees' Time Allocated to Productive Work

Much of the MIS long-range plan is devoted to estimation and allocation of personnel. Each employee engages in many activities that do not contribute directly to corporate profit: breaks, education, daydreaming, restroom breaks, non-work-related discussions, and so on. The planner does not have one person-year to allocate for each person. He or she must establish a percent of employees' time allocated to productive work. As a rule of thumb, this figure should be no higher than 75% and only in rare cases should it be less than 50%. The planner should remember that one employee does not represent one person-year of effort. For example, three people at 65% represents only two person-years of effort that can be allocated to projects—a very important consideration.

Planning: Proactive or Reactive?

A fundamental question must be addressed: Should information services be reactive or proactive? There are advantages to each. Specifically, if a computer center reacts to situations, monies expended for education, systems development, and the like are funneled directly into approved projects. On the other hand, so-called proactive computer centers must commit funds to such activities as professional education and hardware upgrades in anticipation of corporate computing service needs.

There are certain risks that accompany proactive planning. For example, educating all programmers in one type of data-base management system and then selecting noncompatible equipment, for whatever reasons, would result in wasting corporate funds. However, if a need for data-base integration became apparent and all the programmers and analysts needed to gain proficiency on a particular data-base management system (a reactive environment), their efforts would have to be channeled from existing projects, and a certain elapsed time must expire before they are ready to use the data-base management system.

12. It is politically unwise to initiate a project with such widespread influence as an MIS long-range plan without a preliminary explanatory discussion with key persons. User managers with so much at stake would take offense if a planner began the data-gathering activity "cold turkey."

The planner should identify key persons (primarily user and MIS managers and high-level MIS steering committee members) who will be called upon for input and to expend resources. The planner should schedule to meet with these people individually and in groups. If any of the key persons are not already known personally to the planner, the director of MIS should make a special effort to make the necessary introductions. The planner will meet often over a period of months and even years with these people, so the initial interaction should be positive. The formal introduction eliminates the problems associated with making "cold" telephone calls. Remember, people are easily alienated.

The preliminary interview should focus on the purpose and function of an MIS long-range plan. It is the planner's responsibility to ensure that they have an understanding of the scope and importance of the MIS long-range plan and how it will affect their respective areas of responsibility.

An ongoing problem in the development and operation of information systems has been the user's lack of a firm commitment of resources and to approved schedules. Since such commitments are paramount to successful MIS long-range planning, the planner should take this opportunity to discuss why commitments by user and MIS personnel are critical. The planner should impress on both user and MIS managers that for the plan to be successful, commitments must be kept. The plan is actually a document that coordinates commitments and resources. If one manager reneges on his or her commitment, the abilities of others to meet their commitments are affected. The problem snowballs until the plan has no validity and chaos results. It is imperative to obtain not only the cooperation of key personnel, but their understanding of the necessity of commitment.

13. A parallel function of these introductory discussions (Block 12) is to establish and maintain a managerial support base for the MIS long-range plan. This can be done by making those affected aware of the benefits of the plan (see Chapter 1). This support base should be established prior to any effort to gather data or obtain feedback; support is much more difficult to obtain once the planning process has commenced. Subsequent interviews and feedback will help maintain a support base. The planner should ensure that key personnel have a direct link into the MIS planning process, either formal or informal. They also have a right to expect to be informed and updated as to the status of the planning project.

14. The planner has six primary sources from which to gather information: individuals, committees, written documents, vendors, similar companies, and the literature.

Individuals

The planner should interview, on an ongoing basis, persons at various levels of the corporation who are either directly or indirectly involved with information services. These people can provide feedback to the planning process by suggesting alternatives, offering compromises, and/ or discussing trade-offs. The planning process is an iterative procedure that requires constant feedback from all involved or affected.

On occasion the planner may wish to interview personnel at the operational and clerical level. To preserve the political integrity of the MIS planning process, the planner should clear such interviews with the functional area managers.

Even though the MIS long-range planning committee is made up of MIS managers, other personnel within information services have meaningful feedback and should be included in the planner's interview schedule. In one instance planning was limited to the director of MIS and two top MIS managers. Their primary input was from user managers and corporate officers; therefore, the orientation of the plan was application systems. A few candid interviews with programmers and analysts would have brought to light a serious morale and motivation problem. The company's inability to meet deadlines and produce high-quality information systems was rooted in their lack of attention and planning in the area of personnel.

Committees

The high-level MIS steering committee (ISPC) can be queried as a body. If such a committee does not exist, its formation should be included in the MIS long-range plan (see Chapter 7). The ISPC can offer substantial and meaningful input into the planning process. Future application systems requirements, systems integration, and priorities should be the emphasis of the planner's interaction with the ISPC.

The MIS long-range planning committee, comprised of MIS managers, should be the primary source of ideas and also serve as a sounding board for the planner. The planner should meet with this committee at regular intervals (no less than once per month) during the planning process.

Other corporate and MIS committees have valuable input. For example, within MIS the hardware/software acquisition committee, the grievance committee, the system review committee, and others are a continuing source of information. Within the corporation, the executive committee and the personnel committee may provide insight.

Written Documents

The typical MIS department has numerous written documents that can be helpful in the planning process. For example:

Procedures for service requests submittal, I/O distribution, and so on
Postimplementation reviews and periodic system evaluations
Previous MIS long-range plans
MIS documentation and procedures manual
Internal directives
Important memorandums
Department newsletters
Appropriate application systems documentation (including user's manuals)
MIS department organization charts
MIS position descriptions
Internal and external auditors' reports
Other printed matter (depending on company type)

The planner should also seek out similar printed matter at the corporate level and in the functional areas. Of particular importance at the corporate level are the corporate long-range plan, internal policy statements, the corporate organizational chart, directives, manuals, and corporate reports. In the functional areas, the planner should look for anything that might be of assistance in the planning process: an organizational chart, a statement of goals and objectives, an internal procedures manual, and so on.

Vendors

Hardware and software vendors are another valuable source of information. Most marketing representatives are more than happy to become involved in the planning process, especially when there is a possibility that they may reap benefits. Hardware and software planning represent major segments of the MIS long-range plan. Vendors can provide important information on their products and will usually work within the structure of the organization to propose what they feel to be feasible alternative solutions. These solutions are presented in the form of a formal proposal. Vendors are also happy to recommend that you visit successful installations. The planner should either call or visit MIS professionals at these installations to validate the contents of the vendor's proposal(s).

Similar Companies

Other computing centers in similar and even dissimilar industries represent another source of information. Through interaction with a company that has gained experience in certain planning areas, the planner can gain insight that will aid in planning and perhaps allow the planner to avoid certain pitfalls. Another benefit of this type of interaction is the possibility of technology transfer (e.g., system design, software, etc.). Fortunately, of all the major corporate entities, perhaps personnel in the MIS area are those most prone to cooperate with those from another company. The planner will not only glean immediate information, but may develop valuable long-term relationships with sister corporations.

Literature

The volatile and growing field of computers and information systems has spawned many excellent technical periodicals: *Computerworld, Infosystems, Datamation, Data Management*, and *Interface*, to mention a few. These periodicals have numerous articles to spur the imagination of the planner. The best utilization of these periodicals and journals is to scan them for alternative approaches to a solution or for new ideas relative to a particular MIS planning area. It is critical that the planner stay abreast of emerging technology by making a special effort to read periodicals and appropriate MIS books as part of the planning function.

15. At this point in the planning process the planner must evaluate the current status of the corporate information services function and identify the constraints that affect the scope and direction of the planning effort.

Evaluation of Current Status

The purpose of evaluating the current status of the MIS function is to provide the planner with a definition, or "benchmark," of where the information services department stands with respect to the many areas of MIS planning. Compiling an MIS long-range plan is difficult enough when you know where you stand. An effective plan is almost impossible without this benchmark activity. An MIS director and planner may think that he or she has a current and thorough knowledge of all areas of MIS operation, but a close examination will inevitably be revealing. During the evaluation the planner will find many deficiencies, even in well-run MIS shops. The planner must exhibit patience to refrain from thinking about approaches for solutions to these deficiencies. This comes later, once all the cards are on the table.

Before engaging in the MIS long-range planning activity, the planner should evaluate and establish benchmarks related to the status of at least those areas listed below. Neither the list of areas nor the accompanying questions are exhaustive. The areas are presented so that the planner will have a point of departure for the initial evaluation and the questions are examples of representative questions that should be asked by the planner. Part III of this book, Planning Areas, presents hundreds of ideas, questions, approaches and strategies that will prompt the planner to ask other questions necessary to evaluate the current status.

Goals
   Do MIS long-range goals exist?

Are they formally documented?

Are the goals consistent with corporate goals?

Does MIS policy support MIS goals?

Who sets goals?

Who approves goals?

Are established goals sufficiently encompassing?

MIS organization and staff

Is an MIS organizational chart available and up to date?

Does the organizational chart provide for career development?

Is MIS properly staffed?

Are position descriptions available and up to date?

Personnel expertise

Is existing staff, technical and managerial, competent enough to meet objectives?

Do personnel capabilities complement their positions?

Does deadwood exist?

Morale

What is the level of morale within information services?

Is morale causing retention problems?

Systems development methodology

Does a methodology exist?

Is its use encouraged?

Is it used?

How effective is it?

Are documentation procedures and a project management system integrated into the methodology?

Is user interaction built into the methodology?

Operations and controls

Is operations meeting production schedules?

Is there a clear definition of responsibilities for control of systems?

Is the segregation-of-duties maxim followed?

Standards and procedures

Do standard procedures exist for most common MIS activities?

Do people adhere to these procedures?

Are the procedures up to date?

Are standardized procedures presented in an understandable format?

Physical facilities

Is the working space for MIS personnel adequate?

Are an adequate number of conference rooms available?

Are remote hardware locations physically secure?

Planning activities

Is a disaster/contingency plan on file?

Were recommendations of the most recent planning effort followed?

Was the plan evaluated for effectiveness?

Are users an integral part of the MIS planning process?

Does existing MIS planning support corporate long-range plans?

Funds flow

Is funding of information services a problem?

Is information services receiving its fair share during budgeting?

Immediate- and long-term priorities

Have priorities been established for approved budgets?

Who sets priorities?

Are priorities changed at the whim of corporate managers?

Are priorities followed?

Existing software and its quality

Does the existing level of the operating system utilize the hardware to its fullest?

Have some production systems outlived their usefulness?

Are attempts being made to integrate functionally adjacent systems?

Existing hardware and its quality

Is the hardware cost-effective relative to today's standards?

Is vendor support adequate?

Is a hardware upgrade imminent?

Is sufficient backup available to accommodate a disaster?

Security

When was the last comprehensive security analysis completed?

Do unauthorized personnel have access to personal data and information?

External and internal relations

Do existing production systems support a good customer/client relationship?

Is the internal corporate image of MIS positive or negative?

Capacity Assessment

What is the capacity of the information services department to be responsive to users?

Are personnel, budget, and machine capacity documented for now and in the foreseeable future?

Have those items and/or persons that are underutilized or saturated been identified?

Note: Figures 5-1 and 5-2 illustrate machine and budget capacity over a two-year period. Figure 5-1, the Processor Utilization Chart, illustrates present and expected utilization of all central processors. Similar charts could be accomplished for other key hardware devices such as mass storage devices. Most vendors can provide "semireliable" estimates of relative capacities, especially for processors within their own line. Relative capacities for peripheral devices are based on storage capacity and/or input/output speed, as appropriate.

To construct a Processor Utilization Chart, determine the relative capaci-

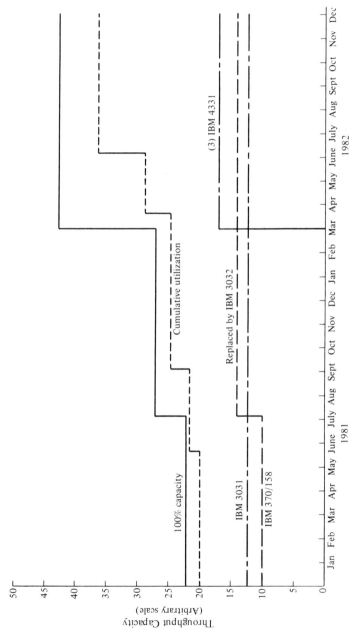

Figure 5-1. *Processor Utilization Chart.*

46

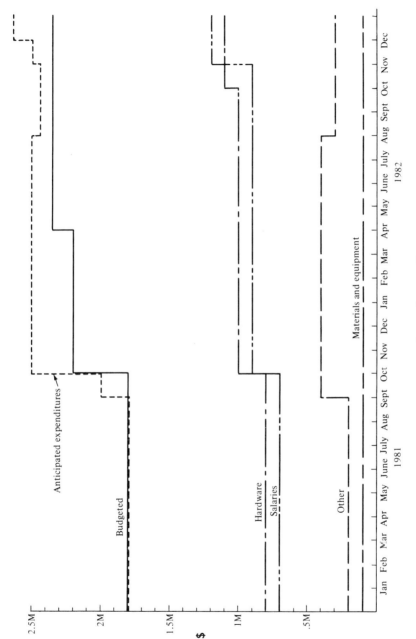

Figure 5-2. Budget Utilization Chart.

ties of the various central processing units. An arbitrary unit can be used based on throughput and/or cycle time. Plot existing and anticipated capacity by processor. Draw a cumulative 100% capacity line and a cumulative utilization line. The chart illustrated in Figure 5-1 reflects a company that presently has an IBM 370/158 and an IBM 3031. The IBM 370/158 will be replaced by an IBM 3032 in July 1981. Three IBM 4331s are scheduled to be implemented in February 1982. Hardware requirements should be based on expected needs shown in the Project Sheduling Chart (Figure 5-9). The dashed line is the actual and/or expected utilization. Again, the expected utilization should be coordinated with expected system testing and implementation dates. The planner may elect to prepare a Processor Utilization Chart for each processor rather than combine capacities.

Figure 5-2, the Budget Utilization Chart, is a tool for graphically illustrating utilization of existing budget and that which is expected. Many computer centers have some flexibility in budget because they have the capacity to generate funds through chargebacks to users. These charges are predictable to a certain extent. The solid line illustrates the expected MIS budget and the dashed line illustrates the anticipated expenditures. Categories are shown on the same chart by using different dash-dot configurations to represent salaries, hardware, materials and supplies, and other (travel, seminar fees, etc.).

At a minimum, the planner should address the areas outlined above and ask these and other questions necessary to evaluate fully and establish benchmarks for the current status of the information services department.

The planner, in cooperation with MIS managers and users, would examine each of the areas described above. The examination results reflect an objective description of the existing MIS function with some qualitative assessments where appropriate. This "status" information serves as input to the planning process. For example, during the evaluation the planner would obtain copies of the most recent MIS organization chart and position descriptions. If either or both are out of date or did not exist, the planner would note these areas for attention during the planning process. As another example, the planner would collect all written standards and procedures, whether used or not, and make some assessment as to their applicability and the extent of their use and acceptance. Also, the planner would inventory physical facilities used or available to MIS. The use of each room, building, and so on, should be described, noting appropriate statistics such as number of offices, number of square feet per nonmanagerial employee, machine room size, location of remote sites, and so on. Other areas would be evaluated in a similar manner.

Identification of Planning Constraints

The identification of the planning constraints is actually a by-product of the evaluation of the current status. As the planner investigates each of the areas listed above, anything that would be expected to limit the scope or direction of the planning effort should be noted. For example, a corporate freeze on hiring over the next year would be a constraint, as would a finite and saturated office space.

The Resultant Product

The end product of the evaluation would be a written report depicting the current status of the information services department and the identification of MIS planning constraints.

16. A written report that details what the planner believes to be the current status of the information services department and identifies constraints to the planning activity is submitted to the MIS long-range planning committee for further scrutiny. The committee should check the accuracy of objective status information, ensure that the planner's quality assessments are an accurate reflection, and validate the constraints. The committee can either approve or reject the report.

If the committee rejects the evaluation, the committee chairman should relay the committee's reservation to the planner both orally and via a formal written memorandum. A rejection could be for a minor point or clarification, for additions necessary to make the report comprehensive, or for major revisions.

An approved status report provides the foundation for the MIS long-range planning effort. Such a report will almost certainly contain sensitive information; therefore, access to the report should be limited to those with a need to know.

17. After receiving a rejection memo detailing the MIS long-range planning committee's reservations about the status report, the planner would interact with the committee to ensure a mutual understanding of what needs to be accomplished, then make the revisions necessary to make the report accurate and comprehensive.

18. The planner has not yet made any effort to plan activities for the future. The planner has resolved certain basic planning issues, developed a support base, initiated the information-gathering effort, compiled a report reflecting the current status of the information services department and constraints to the planning activity, and is now ready to begin planning for the future. The next, and perhaps most important step in the process is to establish goals for MIS over the planning horizon.

Approach to Goals Setting

An MIS long-range plan is simply a document describing a realistic path to attain the goals set forth by the MIS management team (director of MIS, MIS managers, and planner). The team should strive to state MIS goals in general terms that are not subject to interpretation—not an easy task. They should always be cognizant that MIS goals are subordinate and in support of corporate goals.

Definition of MIS goals is the responsibility of the MIS management team. One approach to setting MIS goals is for the director of MIS to prepare an agenda of appropriate goal categories. For example:

Scope and quality of service
Personnel

Organization
Career development and training
MIS image
Policy
Other topics as appropriate

The director then calls a series of meetings of the MIS management team to discuss and resolve MIS goals with respect to each of the preestablished categories.

The setting of goals is a thought-provoking and complex process that cannot be hurried to completion. The process involves reflecting on the past, assessing the present, and predicting the future. For these reasons, the "goals" meetings should be convened on weekends to avoid the interruptions of routine MIS production work. The following is a suggested format for a goals meeting.

Meet on consecutive Saturday mornings at a nonwork location until the goals are finalized and documented. For some reason, meeting at a corporate location tends to channel the discussion to routine activities rather than prompting the abstract thought necessary for goals setting.

Devote the first session to assessing the quality and level of future resource requirements (see Future Resource Requirements below).

In subsequent sessions, discuss agenda items (no more than three per session).

Limit each session to five hours, perhaps 7 A.M. to noon (including breakfast).

Hold this series of goals meetings every one and a half to two years.

Managers should be forewarned of a common pitfall. The typical manager is deeply concerned with deadlines and routine activities and will press to be heard on these issues. "Goals" meetings are not the place for such discussions. It is encumbent upon the director of MIS to keep the meeting objectives in mind and to work toward those objectives.

Since the MIS long-range plan details the activities necessary to attain the MIS goals, the goals should be included in the resultant MIS long-range plan.

Future Resource Requirements

An MIS long-range plan is the framework by which resource requirements are estimated and resources are allocated to specific activities. Because of this, an examination of the quality and level of resource requirements over the planning horizon will provide insight into the goals-setting process. Resources may be categorized into hardware, software, budget, personnel, and data communications. The team should note that these resources are not necessarily independent and that other categories are possible.

Figure 5-3 illustrates an approach that the MIS management team can use to determine the quality and level of resource requirements in the future. Goals are then set based on these requirements.

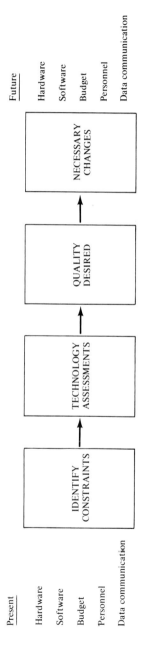

Figure 5-3. Estimating future resource requirements.

51

The evaluation of the current status of the information services department (Block 15) provides the MIS management team with a benchmark from which to begin. With a knowledge of the present level and quality of resources, the first step is to isolate, from those planning constraints identified in Block 15, the procedural, monetary, operational, political, and time constraints that have a bearing on the goals-setting process. These constraints are noted in order to eliminate the possibility of having to backtrack because of a violation to a previously unidentified constraint. For example, the personnel department may have issued an eighteen-month hiring freeze on professional personnel. Another example would be a known budget over the next two years.

Having identified appropriate constraints to goals setting, the next step is to make a technological assessment. This is a difficult task and requires that the MIS management team make a forecast of future technological developments over the horizon of the plan. Unfortunately, this must be done with limited information. A corporation that elects to follow a trend that is not supported by hardware and software vendors may find MIS personnel doing expensive development and maintenance work unnecessarily. For example, to support this unique environment, systems programmers may be required to make major modifications to vendor-supplied operating systems.

The next step is to establish a desired level of quality for each resource. To say that all areas within the realm of MIS should be of the highest quality is unrealistic. Trade-offs must be considered and compromises must be made. No corporation has unlimited resources. The quality issue can be addressed as a compromise between that which is ideal and that which is practical. An MIS long-range plan developed at either end of the spectrum is doomed to failure. The effective MIS plan promotes the ideal, but is tempered by the limitations of that which is practical.

Once the MIS management team has arrived at a consensus of what the future environment should be, they should describe, in general, what changes are necessary in the various areas of MIS in order to achieve the projected future resource requirements. For example, the team should answer such questions as: What changes in organizational structure are required? What existing application system areas should be integrated? The responses to these and many other questions will involve the initiation of some type of MIS activity. The identification, planning, and scheduling of these project-oriented and ongoing activities is the backbone of the MIS long-range planning process.

19. A "comprehensive" MIS long-range plan is advocated in this book. A comprehensive plan focuses attention on virtually all areas that affect the MIS function. Planning in some areas discussed in this book has been neglected by many information services departments. An MIS long-range plan that encompasses less than the topic areas discussed in Part III of this book will give less than adequate coverage to the considerations necessary for MIS planning.

For whatever reason, some computer centers may elect to be less comprehensive in their planning. The contents of MIS long-range plans vary considerably from one corporation to the next. This book addresses the major areas of MIS planning that are appropriate for virtually every corporation. The planner should not only select areas from those presented in this book, but add others that are critical to developing the most effective plan for their corporation.

At the onset of planning for the future, the planner, in cooperation with the MIS long-range committee, should identify all areas that affect MIS operation. The planner, with the assistance of the director of MIS, should then identify those areas that are critical to MIS planning. By doing this, the planner can focus attention on those high-priority areas if cost and personnel constraints preclude the development of a "comprehensive" MIS long-range plan.

Possible topical areas for an MIS long-range plan are listed below:

Policy (Chapter 7)
Application systems (Chapter 8)
Hardware (Chapter 9)
Systems software (Chapter 10)
MIS structural organization (Chapter 11)
Personnel (Chapter 12)
Management (Chapter 13)
Operations (Chapter 14)
Standardization of documentation and procedures (Chapter 15)
Productivity improvement (Chapter 16)
Facilities (Chapter 17)
Contingency planning (Chapter 18)
Social impact and legal implications (Chapter 19)
MIS image (Chapter 20)
Word processing and office automation (Chapter 21)
Costs (Chapter 22)
Other, depending on type industry (i.e., R&D)

The topics listed above correspond to chapter titles in Part III. Depending on the prevailing MIS environment, several less apparent topic areas could also be included. For example:

Forecast of future MIS environment
Identification of MIS strengths and weaknesses
Forecast of future corporate industry environment

20. Once the plan content areas have been determined, the MIS Planning Matrix can be completed. The function of the Planning Matrix is to encourage the planner to consider the interactions between the various planning areas. The planner, the MIS long-range planning committee, and the director of MIS should have an awareness of how planning for one area affects planning for another. The Planning Matrix of Figure 5-4 illustrates which planning areas affect or overlap each other.

	1 Policy	2 Application system	3 Hardware	4 Systems software	5 Organization	6 Personnel (including education)	7 Management	8 Operation	9 Documentation and procedure	10 Productivity	11 Facilities	12 Contingency planning	13 Social and legal	14 Image	15 Word processing and office automation
1 Policy	■	←	X		X	X		←				X	X		←
2 Application systems		■	←	X		↑		X	X			X			
3 Hardware			■	←		↑		X		←		X		X	←
4 Systems software				■		↑		X				X			X
5 Organization					■	←					←	X			
6 Personnel (including education)						■	X		X	X	X			X	
7 Management							■		X	X	X				
8 Operations								■		X		X		X	X
9 Documentation and procedures									■	←	X				X
10 Productivity										■	X				X
11 Facilities											■	X		X	X
12 Contingency planning												■			
13 Social and legal													■	X	
14 Image														■	
15 Word processing and office automation															■

X — Planning for one impacts planning for the other

← — Prerequisite to planning area noted

Figure 5-4. MIS Planning Matrix.

Each planning area discussed in Part III interacts with at least one of the other areas. For example, a proposed systems software upgrade may affect hardware acquisition, the in-house education program, and application systems planning.

To complete the Planning Matrix, the planner would conduct a brainstorming session with the MIS Long-Range Planning Committee. The objectives of this session would be to note potential interactions and to accompany each interaction pair with a short word description listing the manner or type of interactions. An "X" is placed in the appropriate matrix block to indicate that one planning area has a direct impact on the other. If one planning area is a prerequisite to the other, an arrow points to the prerequisite. As an example, in Figure 5-4, applications systems planning is noted as a prerequisite to hardware planning. An interaction is also noted between personnel and facilities because expected growth in personnel would have a direct impact on space requirements. The interactions noted in Figure 5-4 are included primarily to illustrate the mechanics of preparing the MIS Planning Matrix. They should not be construed as typical interactions. The scope of the MIS planning effort, the planning areas selected, and the maturity and sophistication of the existing MIS environment will significantly alter the complexion of the MIS Planning Matrix from one corporation to the next.

For each interaction pair noted on the Planning Matrix, the planner would list and explain the points of interaction. These accompanying descriptions are part of the MIS Planning Matrix.

A by-product of the process of identifying the interaction between the various planning areas is that the planner and the MIS Long-Range Planning Committee are encouraged to think abstractly about the various areas of MIS operation. Ideas and approaches to solutions of existing problems often result. Also, completion of the MIS Planning Matrix ensures that the planner has "covered all the bases."

21. After the planner has completed the matrix and accompanying written descriptions of interactions, the MIS Long-Range Planning Committee ensures that the documentation is an accurate and complete reflection of previous discussions.

The chairman of the committee should document the committee's decision via an approval or rejection memorandum to the planner. If the matrix and accompanying descriptions are rejected, the memorandum should note discrepancies.

22. The planner makes the necessary revisions according to the rejection memorandum and resubmits the MIS Planning Matrix and accompanying documentation to the MIS Long-Range Planning Committee.

23. This structured approach to MIS planning reduces the complex MIS planning process to more easily intelligible and manageable modules (planning areas). What needs to be addressed with respect to each planning area is a function of the corporation's MIS sophistication, maturity, and corporation type. The planner would examine what needs to be done (considering all interactions), set objectives, then decide how to go about achieving these objectives.

Part III of this book, Planning Areas, presents ideas, approaches, solutions, and strategies for planning in each of the major areas of MIS.

24. Since resources are scheduled and allocated by activity, the planner must identify the specific activities necessary to carry out the planning objectives set forth in Block 23. In every computer center there are essentially two types of MIS activities. These activities can be classified as either project oriented (one-time) or ongoing (recurring) activities. The MIS long-range planner would list those ongoing and project-oriented activities necessary to meet planning objectives. Ongoing activities are often the result of project-oriented activities.

25. The planner lists all project-oriented activities. Once a project is completed, the activity is terminated. The list should include not only proposed projects, but activities that are expected to be completed over the MIS long-range plan horizon. The following are examples of project-oriented activities:

Feasibility studies
Application systems development
Conversion and implementation of application systems (often considered part of the development project)
Periodic system reviews
Internal and external audits
Security audits and/or risk analyses
Development of documentation and procedures manual (and other in-house manuals)
Major system enhancements
System software upgrades
Education (group or individual)
Construction or physical facilities improvement
Hardware/software acquisition
Equipment installation
Cost/benefit analysis of an activity

26. The planner lists all proposed and current ongoing activities. Examples of ongoing activities are:

Production and control of an application system (list each separately—e.g., payroll, inventory, general ledger, etc.)
Minor enhancements to application systems—general maintenance (list each separately—e.g., payroll, inventory, general ledger, etc.)
Administration and management of the MIS function
MIS long-range planning
Writing, publishing, and distributing monthly MIS department newsletter

27. At least one week prior to a committee meeting, the planner submits a list of proposed and current activities to the MIS Long-Range Planning Committee for evaluation. During the meeting the planner should present the logic and justification for the selection of the activities.

The MIS Long-Range Planning Committee evaluates the planner's list of proposed and current activities. The committee should pay particular attention to whether or not all current activities are listed. The proposed activities should be complete and accurately reflect the planning necessary in the various MIS planning areas. In addition, the committee should check to see that the planner has integrated and combined overlapping and functionally adjacent activities.

A rejection or an approval of the planner's list of activities should be reflected in a memorandum from the committee chairman to the planner. The purpose of the memorandum is to document the committee's concerns and any revisions requested by the committee.

28. After the planner receives a memorandum rejecting the list of activities, the planner revises the list as required and resubmits it to the MIS Long-Range Planning Committee.

29. The technical and economic feasibility of some of the proposed activities may be debatable. The planner and the director of MIS should identify those activities and schedule someone (not necessarily the planner) to perform the necessary feasibility studies.

30. Feasibility studies are conducted on those activities whose economic and/or technical feasibility is questionable. Those persons accomplishing the feasibility studies should keep in mind that the results of these studies are primarily for use in the MIS long-range planning effort. The director of MIS and the MIS long-range planner are seeking general, not specific, input into the planning process. The marginal returns for accomplishing comprehensive feasibility studies at this stage are not justified. A minimum of effort should be expended to determine the economic and technical feasibility of these activities.

31. The planner revises the activities list based on the results of the feasibility studies.

32. The planner, with input from the MIS Long-Range Planning Committee, selects the optimum mixture of MIS activities. Limited resources are available to realize the implementation of the complete list of ongoing and project-oriented activities compiled from investigating the various MIS planning areas (Block 23). Therefore, to optimize the mixture of activities for the good of the corporation, the planner must delete some proposed activities. This mixture can be determined by selecting the proper ratio of project-oriented and ongoing activities and the mixture of high- and low-risk activities. Those activities identified by the director of MIS as being critical and therefore of high priority are a "given" in the activities selection process.

Based on the considerations and procedures discussed below, the planner compiles a list of project-oriented and ongoing activities to be incorporated into the MIS long-range plan.

Ratio of Project-Oriented to Ongoing Activities

The ratio of the personnel time expended on project-oriented activities to the time expended on ongoing activities will probably change markedly after implementation of an MIS long-range plan. For example, if the present ratio is

$$\frac{\text{project}}{\text{ongoing}} = \frac{1}{2}$$

expect the ratio to increase substantially after plan implementation—perhaps to

$$\frac{\text{project}}{\text{ongoing}} = \frac{2}{1}$$

A change of this magnitude will not occur immediately but is a realistic expectation for two years after plan implementation and should be factored into the planning process. A comprehensive MIS long-range plan will decrease the resource requirements for such areas as systems maintenance and MIS management. Because of this, the planner has the flexibility to divert resources to needed activities (probably those that affect responsiveness to users).

Risk and MIS Projects

Each existing and proposed project should be given some type of rating relative to risk. The risk refers to the validity of the personnel, money, and time estimates, and to the probability of project completion. To select and propose all high-risk projects would jeopardize the success of the MIS department and the company. On the other hand, across-the-board selection of low-risk projects would probably eliminate certain needed projects from consideration. The best approach is to select an optimal mixture of high- and low-risk projects. Each project should be evaluated relative to complexity, level of technology required, and scope.

Those projects that are highly structured provide the project coordinator with a clear view of what needs to be done. These projects will have a low to medium risk, depending upon whether the project is of high or low technology and/or a small or large project. Similarly, the projects that do not have a clear beginning and end will have a medium to high risk. An example of a low-risk project would be the introduction of a series of in-house seminars on data-base management systems. An example of a high-risk project would be the implementation of an integrated on-line materials requirements planning system.

Figure 5-5 illustrates graphically the proper mixture of high- and low-risk MIS projects. The "proper" area would vary about the center depending upon the venturesome nature of the corporation (willingness to accept risk).

To use the Evaluation Matrix of Figure 5-6, the planner and members of the MIS Long-Range Planning Committee would first identify the projects to be evalu-

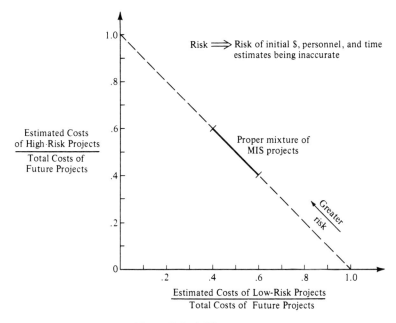

Figure 5-5. *MIS project mix.*

ated and list them at the top of each column. Next, they would establish criteria for risk evaluation and list the criteria with the relative risk importance (portion of 100%) on the rows. Note that complexity, level of technology, and scope are only suggested criteria. Each person would rate a project by each criterion relative to project risk. For example, if Project 1 was extremely unstructured and complex, an evaluator might rate the project risk as 38 of 40 (highest risk). If Project 1 was within the corporate technological expertise and was limited in size and scope, the evaluator might give the project a 10 of 30 rating for technology and 15 of 30 rating for scope. The total risk of Project 1 for one evaluator might be 38 + 10 + 15 = 63, an overall medium level of risk. Every evaluator would go through the same exercise for each project and the results would be combined to form a consensus risk evaluation. See Figure 5-7 for an illustration of a final summary.

Figure 5-8 illustrates the degree of uncertainty that the planner must consider for high- and low-risk project estimates relative to dollar, time, and/or personnel expenditures. For example, if the company selected primarily high-risk projects with a risk curve similar to curve A, the possibility exists that all projects could substantially exceed the budgeted amount, thereby placing a severe hardship on the MIS department and the corporation. On the other hand, a low-risk project with a risk curve similar to curve B will not severely hamper the integrity of the service level of MIS even if the project goes well over budget. It behooves the MIS department not to have an inordinate number of high-risk projects.

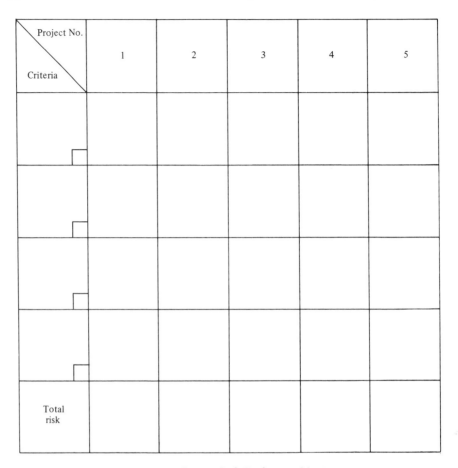

Figure 5-6. Project Risk Evaluation Matrix.

33. The MIS Long-Range Planning Committee evaluates the list of activities proposed by the planner to ensure that they are consistent with corporate objectives and are within the capabilities of the MIS department. Any objections to the proposed list should be detailed in a memorandum to the planner.

34. The planner revises the list of activities to the satisfaction of the MIS Long-Range Planning Committee.

35. The Project Scheduling Chart and the Requirements Planning Chart for Personnel of Figures 5-9 and 5-10 are mechanically easy to compile (Blocks 37 through 40). The difficulty comes in setting project priorities and making personnel and cost estimates (Block 36) with such limited information. The planner, in cooperation with the director of MIS and the MIS Long-Range Planning Committee, can

Project No. / Criteria	No. 1 Upgrade of batch personnel system to online	No. 2 Feasibility study for C550 system	No. 3 Annual security analysis	No. 4 Machine room construction	No. 5 MIS reorganization
Complexity ⟨40⟩	30	35	15	10	15
Use of technology ⟨30⟩	30	20	10	25	5
Scope/Size ⟨30⟩	10	10	10	25	10
Total risk	70	65	35	60	30

Figure 5-7. Example of a Project Risk Evaluation Matrix.

use the following approach to setting priorities. Unless extenuating circumstances prevail, existing projects and ongoing activities would be given the highest priorities. One proven approach to establishing priorities involves collective thinking and decision making on the part of the planner, the director of MIS, and the MIS Long-Range Planning Committee. The planner serves as the leader.

This approach assumes that each person in the group has a knowledge of the problem or task and the ability to provide meaningful rationale to support their opinion on a particular matter of discussion. Considering the above-named participants, this should not be problem. The results of this iterative approach is a group consensus opinion. The steps are as follows:

A. The planner serves as the leader and explains the objective (setting priorities). The planner should also present appropriate considerations in establishing priorities. Possible considerations are:

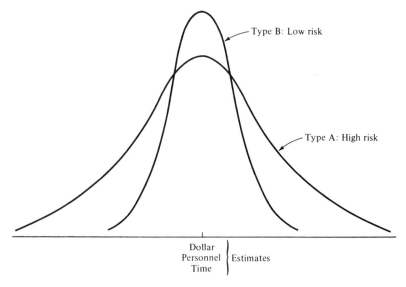

Figure 5-8. *Project risk curves.*

Corporate need [compatibility with major thrusts of corporation and input from the Information Systems Policy Committee (ISPC)]

Availability of critical expertise

Length and complexity of the project

Systems dependencies and integration

Availability of support hardware

Corporate preparedness (physically, educationally, psychologically, etc.)

Opportunity to increase productivity

Portability (potential for use as a standard product in corporate entities with similar objectives)

If necessary, the planner should present appropriate background information.

B. The planner lists all proposed project and ongoing activities for all to see.

C. The planner (and/or director of MIS) may need to clarify why a particular activity is included in the list. If participants indicate that all activities are clear in their initial presentation, this step may be omitted.

D. In this step, each member of the group ranks the activities. Depending on the number of activities initially listed, an odd number somewhat less than the total of the list is selected. For example, seven might be selected from a list of fifteen activities. Each member of the group selects what they believe to be the top seven (in the example case) activities, then assigns a ranking to each activity by starting with the extremes and working to the middle (i.e.,

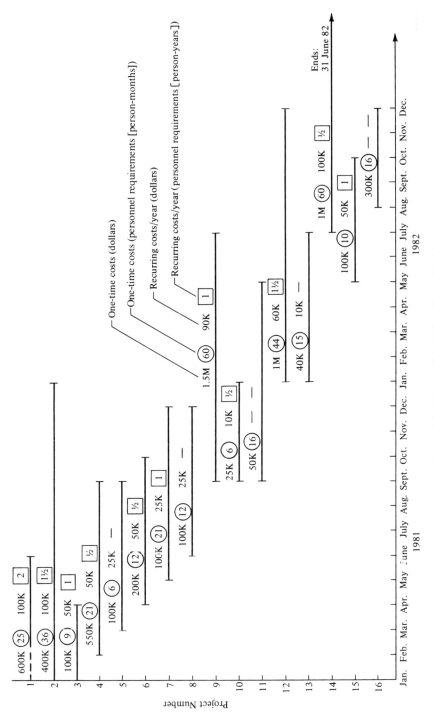

Figure 5-9. Project Scheduling Chart (initial).

63

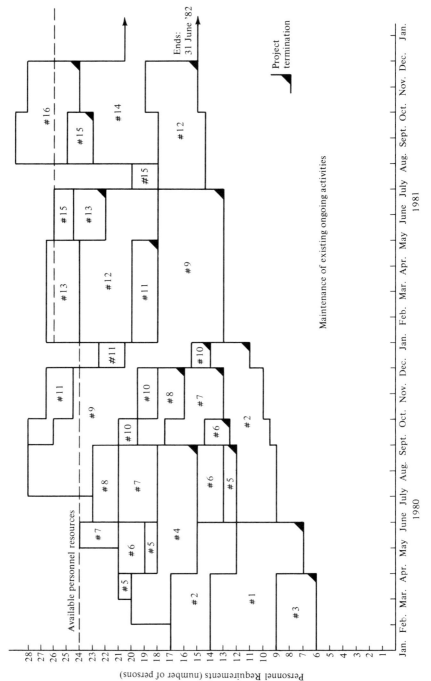

Figure 5-10. Requirements Planning Chart for Personnel (initial).

64

first, seventh, second, sixth, third, fifth, fourth). For ease of tabulation, each person, including the planner, notes the ranking for each activity on a separate card (highest priority item is given a "7").

E. The scores are tabulated. The group ranking for each activity is the total of the individual rankings. The activities are listed in order (most significant first) for all to see.

F. The planner coordinates an open discussion to debate personal differences with the ordered list compiled from accumulated individual rankings.

G. Repeat steps D, E, and F until it is apparent that further iterations will not significantly alter the priorities shown in the most recent ordered list. If executed correctly, this approach has the potential to yield consensus priorities, and thereby render a set of priorities that are acceptable to the MIS management team. Priorities established by the MIS management team, with input from the ISPC, are still subject to final approval by the ISPC.

36. The scheduling process requires that the planner, with input from the MIS Long-Range Planning Committee, make preliminary estimates of costs and personnel requirements for each activity proposed. These estimates are based primarily on a concept and not a design or a comprehensive description of a particular activity. Reasonable estimates of costs and personnel requirements will be available for at least some of the activities from the feasibility studies completed in Block 30.

A procedure similar to the one discussed in Block 35 can be used to make estimates of costs, personnel, and time (as appropriate) requirements. The same MIS personnel are involved and the assumption of knowledgeable participants must be adhered to. The planner is again the leader. The following steps describe an approach to making reasonable estimates:

A. The planner presents the task and appropriate background information.

B. Each participant submits a written estimate (of cost, personnel requirements, or time).

C. The planner plots on a linear scale the estimate of each member of the group.

D. The upper and lower quartiles and the median are calculated and marked on the linear scale.

E. Those participants whose estimates fall in the lower and upper quartiles are asked to explain their rationale for their low or high estimates.

F. The planner coordinates an open discussion based on the estimates plotted.

G. Repeat steps B through F until the returns for increasing the accuracy of the estimate do not merit another iteration. The dispersion of the estimates should be reduced with each iteration.

H. The estimate is the median or the mean (as appropriate). The dispersion of the estimate is an indication of the risk involved. See Figure 5-8, Project Risk Curves.

37. The preparation of the Project Scheduling Chart (Figure 5-9) is an iterative process. The scheduling process is essentially a trade-off between maintaining the priorities set in Block 35 and minimizing the fluctuation in personnel requirements (work-load leveling). Given priorities, costs, and personnel requirements (Blocks 35 and 36), the planner prepares a preliminary Project Scheduling Chart. Depending on the personnel commitment at any given time, the planner has some latitude in selecting the duration of the project; however, priorities, costs, and personnel requirements are fixed. The planner should be aware that the termination of a project activity often marks the beginning of an ongoing activity.

As shown in Figure 5-9, Project 1, a market analysis system is presently underway and scheduled to be completed at the end of May. Project 4, the development of a materials requirements planning (MRP) system, is scheduled to begin February 1 and to be completed at the end of August. The MRP project will require 21 person-months of effort over the life of the project from February 1 to September 1. This is indicated by a circled 21. The estimated dollar expenditure for Project 4 is $550,000. This amount represents the estimated total one-time project cost— materials, machine time, personnel, and so on. The "½" in the square represents the estimated recurring costs in person-years per year over the life of the project. In most cases the recurring costs begin immediately after project termination (usually system implementation). The $50,000 represents the annual recurring costs (maintenance and production) of the proposed MRP system.

38. After the planner has developed a preliminary Project Scheduling Chart for all existing and proposed projects, the planner can then use a Requirements Planning Chart for Personnel, as shown in Figure 5-10, to prepare a more efficient schedule. The dashed line on the Requirements Planning Chart for Personnel indicates the level of available personnel resources at any given point in time. It is important that personnel be scheduled at or no more than slightly above the existing staffing level (maximum of 5% above) unless an adequate supply of competent temporary assistance is available at a reasonable cost. If the chart indicates an extraordinary personnel requirement or underutilization (10% above or below staffing level) over a given month or quarter, the Project Scheduling Chart should be revised to level the work load, and therefore personnel requirements, over time. This is the case in Figure 5-10. The planner should note that, for any given project, requirements at any given point in time may vary considerably over the life of the project. A more detailed Project Scheduling Chart for Personnel, showing variations in personnel requirements over time for a particular project, can be accomplished at a later date. Typically, this would be too much detail for an MIS long-range plan.

The planner will probably have to go through several iterations of the Project Scheduling Chart and the accompanying Requirements Planning Chart for Personnel to level the work load. Although personnel and dollar estimates are fixed, the planner has some flexibility to either lengthen or shorten the duration of a project and/or to shift the project completion date forward or backward in time. When the shifting of a completion date alters the relative priorities of projects, the planner should clear such changes with the director of MIS. Figures 5-11 and 5-12 show the

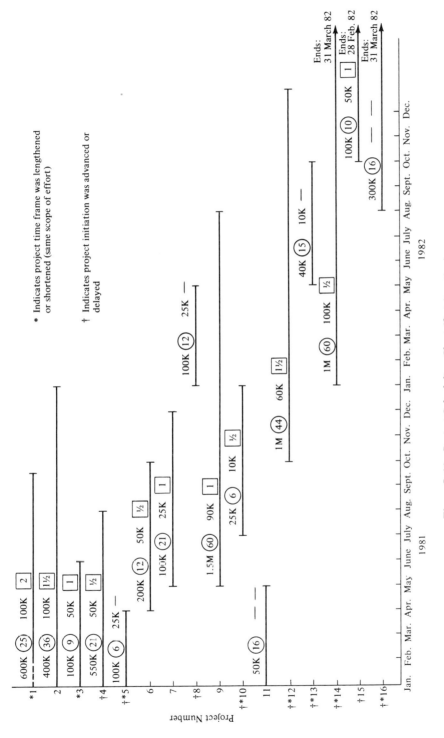

Figure 5-11. *Project Scheduling Chart (first iteration).*

67

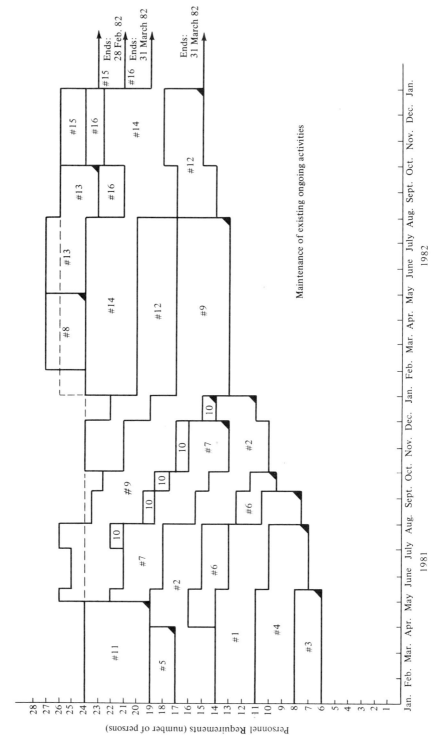

Figure 5-12. Requirements Planning Chart for Personnel (first iteration).

first iteration and a more acceptable schedule. Typically, two or more iterations will be required to derive a workable schedule. This iterative process is easily computerized. The planner should note that personnel requirements for ongoing activities are also included in the Requirements Planning Chart for Personnel.

39. If the corporation is not capable of providing a buffer for fluctuations in cash flow to the information services department, a Requirements Planning Chart for Cost, Figure 5-13, can be drawn up and serve as input to the scheduling process. Cash flow analysis is usually not a critical item to MIS long-range planning. The cash flow requirements in the example are exaggerated to illustrate more clearly the Requirements Planning Chart for Cost.

40. Once the long-range planner has compiled a feasible Project Scheduling Chart, the chart is submitted to the MIS Long-Range Planning Committee for review. An oral presentation by the planner would help the committee in their evaluation.

The chairman of the committee would draft a memorandum reflecting the acceptance or rejection of the Project Scheduling Chart. A rejection memorandum should detail the committee's reservations.

41. The Project Scheduling Chart has a direct effect on the functional areas and, therefore, the Information Systems Policy Committee (ISPC). It is encumbent upon the ISPC to evaluate the Project Scheduling Chart with respect to project priorities, completion dates, and the time frames over which the projects will be completed. The Project Scheduling Chart is completed for the corporate good and the ISPC should evaluate it with this in mind. Members of the ISPC will have individual biases, but the acceptance or rejection of the proposed Project Scheduling Chart should reflect a consensus by the ISPC. This consensus is critical to the implementation of the MIS long-range plan.

The chairman of the ISPC prepares a memorandum reflecting the acceptance or rejection of the proposed Project Scheduling Chart. In the case of rejection, the reservations and proposed revisions should be noted.

42. The planner makes the necessary revisions to the Project Scheduling Chart and resubmits it to the ISPC for evaluation.

43. With the ISPC acceptance of the Project Scheduling Chart, the planner is given an official go-ahead to prepare the details for implementation of the proposed activities. This means that the planner can begin the preparation of the written MIS long-range plan. The first step in the preparation of the written plan is to select the section headings and prepare a very general outline of the plan. An example outline is shown in Figure 5-14.

The general outline of the written MIS long-range plan provides a framework from which the planner can begin the task of filling in the details.

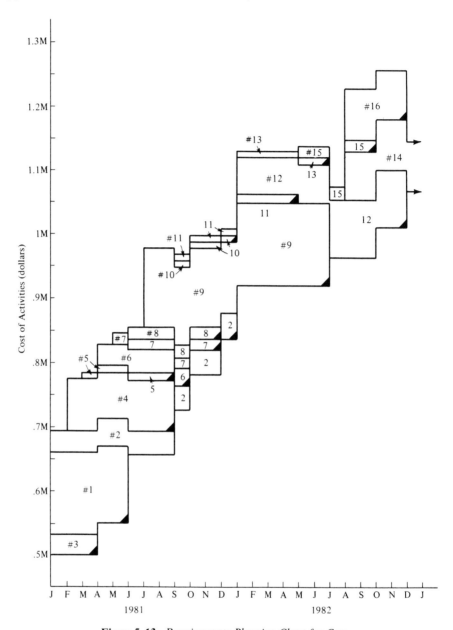

Figure 5-13. *Requirements Planning Chart for Cost.*

44. The planner prepares the MIS long-range plan. The MIS long-range plan contains the details for accomplishing the proposed activities over the horizon of the plan. The plan reflects changes, approaches, potential problems and solutions, and

EXECUTIVE SUMMARY
INTRODUCTION
GOALS
CURRENT MIS STATUS
PLANNING CONSTRAINTS
MIS POLICY
PLANNING AREAS
    APPLICATION SYSTEMS
    HARDWARE
    SYSTEMS SOFTWARE
    ORGANIZATION
    PERSONNEL
    OPERATION AND PRODUCTION
    STANDARDIZATION OF PROCEDURES
    PRODUCTIVITY
    FACILITIES
    OFFICE AUTOMATION
    INTERNAL RELATIONS
    CONTINGENCY PLANNING
SUMMARY OF PROPOSED ACTIVITIES
BENEFITS/COST SUMMARY
IMPLEMENTATION SCHEDULE AND METHOD
MIS LONG-RANGE PLAN MAINTENANCE PROCEDURES

Figure 5-14.   *Example structure of an MIS long-range plan.*

implementation methods for the proposed activities. The planner's knowledge and the contents of this book can provide input to this process.

45. During the preparation of the MIS long-range plan, the planner should be in constant interaction with users, MIS managers, the ISPC, and the MIS Long-Range Planning Committee. This interaction should be somewhat formalized. A suggested approach is presented in Phase 1, Block 9, and is illustrated in Figure 4-2.

46. Once the planner has completed a draft of the MIS long-range plan, the director of MIS must approve the draft before it is sent to the ISPC for final approval. The director should pay particular attention to the plan's content, style, and organization, and ensure that the written plan is understandable by those with a need to know.

47. The planner revises the draft of the MIS long-range plan to correct what the director of MIS considers to be deficiencies. This "clean up" process may take over a month for medium-sized to large corporations. A plan that cannot be understood has little real value; therefore, whatever time is required to make the plan more presentable is time well spent.

48. A draft of the MIS long-range plan is distributed two weeks in advance of a scheduled ISPC meeting.

49. The planner makes a verbal presentation to the ISPC on the proposed MIS long-range plan.

50. After reading the MIS long-range plan and hearing a verbal presentation on the plan, the ISPC either approves or rejects the proposed plan. The chairman of the ISPC submits a memorandum that reflects the plan's acceptance or rejection. In case of rejection, the memorandum also details the committee's reservations and/or requested changes.

In theory, the MIS director should be completely behind the planner and the MIS long-range plan. The director of MIS, if not on the ISPC, should be present to support and provide justification for controversial aspects of the proposed plan.

51. It is implied that the director of MIS is in agreement with the revisions requested by the ISPC. The planner revises the MIS long-range plan as appropriate.

52. Revisions that have little or no bearing on the scope or basic content of the MIS long-range plan are considered minor. These revisions are made and the MIS long-range plan is submitted directly to the ISPC for approval at the next scheduled meeting.

Revisions that have a significant effect on the scope and/or content of the MIS long-range plan are considered major; therefore, a major rewrite may be required.

53. An ISPC-approved strategic MIS long-range plan is submitted to the chief executive officer of the corporation for approval. The CEO may request a verbal presentation, if needed. Presumably, controversial issues would have been debated and resolved by the ISPC. The CEO should reflect an approval or rejection via a formal memorandum to the MIS long-range planner and the chairman of the ISPC.

Chapter 6

Phase 3: Implementation and Maintenance

With formal approval of the proposed MIS long-range plan, the planner can proceed to compile and distribute the plan. The actual implementation is accomplished by the director of MIS and the MIS management team.

The planning function, and therefore the MIS long-range planner's job, is ongoing. The distribution of a plan marks the beginning of a new planning period.

BLOCK DESCRIPTIONS—PHASE 3

54. An MIS long-range plan, even for a small corporation, is a formidable document, comparable in size, difficulty, and scope to a technical book. Prior to publication, an MIS book has an army of proofreaders, copy editors, and production editors attending to organization, style, continuity, and grammer. The objective of this exercise is not only to make the book grammatically correct and readable, but so that it will be an asset to the potential users. The long-range planner has similar objectives for the MIS long-range plan, but support services are usually limited.

If skills in copy and production editing and graphics are not available within the corporation, the work should be contracted to professionals. A common mistake made by MIS professionals is to write and distribute documents such as MIS long-range plans, user manuals, and so on, without critical input from specialists. Thousands of such documents sit on shelves gathering dust because the authors had an unjustified confidence in their ability to write coherently.

The MIS plan must be geared to the appropriate audience. This is a difficult task because the audience will invariably have a broad range of MIS experiences. Frequent users of the MIS long-range plan will be corporate officers, members of the ISPC, and MIS managers. A quick scan of the audience points out the fact that computerese should be avoided. A plan that cannot be understood by its intended audience has little value and can actually be counterproductive. The MIS function, and therefore the MIS long-range plan, has enormous impact on the direction of the corporation; therefore, no section of the plan should be difficult to read or subject to interpretation.

The physical preparation of the MIS long-range plan can usually be done within the company. The company that does not have text-editing software for written material, a professional draftsman for graphs, charts, and forms, and a print shop can easily find these services available commercially.

The MIS long-range plan is a formal document and should be professionally packaged. The cost is minimal. The binding should be a high-quality multiring (ten or more ring) binder with the title and corporate logo emblazoned on the binder. Preprinted dividers separating the various segments of the plan are also recommended. The ring binder is necessary to accommodate changes.

The planner should be cognizant of the correlation between the quality of the physical product (typing quality, binding, graphics, etc.) and a manager's willingness to adopt or even read the plan. Although a small part of the MIS planning process, the planner must not slight the importance of producing a professional-appearing MIS long-range plan.

A warning is appropriate at this point. Persons not familiar with the compilation of a major document should be advised that the time required to complete the project is usually substantially underestimated. The details of compilation can become overwhelming. Be prepared and schedule for minor delays.

55. The actual distribution of the MIS long-range plan signals the beginning of the implementation process. The planner should cooperate with the director of MIS in determining who should receive copies of the plan. Remember that long-range plans are volatile and must be continuously updated; therefore, unnecessary distribution may result in some plans not being properly updated.

The MIS long-range plan is not a public document. There should be some control to its distribution and availability. The greater the number of copies distributed throughout the corporation, the higher the probability of a plan being read by an individual or group of individuals without a "need to know." A typical MIS long-range plan will contain sensitive and controversial recommendations that can be misconstrued by individuals who do not understand the total scope of the plan. As a rule of thumb, the plan should be distributed to the chief executive officer, each member of the ISPC, other selected user managers (based on the "need to know"), the director of MIS, the director's immediate managers, and the MIS long-range planner.

It is the responsibility of the planner to maintain a distribution log for the initial MIS long-range plan and for subsequent changes. Figures 6-1 illustrates one possible format for such a log. Isolated revisions to the plan are distributed and controlled by the planner, but the full body should not be redistributed more than once per year. When the revisions to the original (or most recent) MIS long-range plan become excessive and inhibit readability, the planner may find it necessary to compile a new MIS long-range plan in a more logical, up to date manner.

Distribution Log for Long-Range Plan												
Person responsible	Department	Initial delivery	Year	1	2	Year	1	2	Year	1	2	
				3	4		3	4		3	4	
Harry Schultz	Comptroller	18 Sept 79	79	⟍	⟍	80	⟍	⟍				
Jack Kent	System Mgr, DP	18 Sept 79	79	⟍	⟍	80	⟍	⟍				
Sally Radford	DP Mgr	20 Sept 80				80	⟍					

Latest Version of MIS Long-Range Plan			
1 1979-1 18 Sept 79	5 1980-3 14 June 80	9	
2 1979-2 1 Dec 79	6	10	
3 1980-1 1 Feb 80	7	11	
4 1980-2 1 May 80	8	12	

Figure 6-1. Distribution log for an MIS long-range plan.

56. Each segment of the MIS long-range plan should have been prepared in cooperation with the Information Systems Policy Committee, MIS managers, and appropriate user managers. If the procedures illustrated in Figure 4-2 (interaction between principles in the MIS long-range planning process) were followed, implementation of the MIS long-range plan should be smooth and present no serious problems. This procedure ensures that trade-offs are considered and that differences are negotiated and resolved prior to implementation.

There are basically four implementation strategies:

1. Demonstration
2. Power and politics
3. Persuasion
4. Involvement

Demonstration

Computer centers developing an MIS long-range plan for the first time do not have an opportunity to demonstrate its effectiveness to in-house personnel. However, other similar corporations have been successful in implementing an MIS long-range plan and most are pleased to demonstrate and discuss their successes. Users and corporate officers must be sold and then resold prior to implementation. The benefits of a long-range plan can be demonstrated through interaction with a company that successfully developed and implemented an MIS long-range plan. Users should be cognizant of the possibility that the scope and format of the proposed plan may be significantly different from the plan being demonstrated. After the first couple of years of in-house MIS long-range planning, the benefits become apparent and the demonstration strategy is continuous, precluding the need for site visits to other companies.

Power and Politics

Every organization has its political structure. In the initial phases of the planning methodology, the planner works to establish an Information Systems Policy Committee, a necessary prerequisite to MIS long-range planning. The ISPC is one approach to soliciting cooperation and creating a power base among supportive users. Power and politics alone are not sufficient to implement all recommendations in an MIS long-range plan; however, the effects of the plan are far-reaching. The planner must be attuned to the corporate political structure and work within it to obtain the support of high-level management.

Persuasion

It is encumbent upon the planner to assist MIS and user management in persuading those affected by the plan of the expected net positive results. The persuasion campaign would be aimed primarily at operational personnel, assuming that higher-level managers are convinced of the merit of the recommendations of the MIS long-range plan. The best approach would be for MIS and user managers to coordinate small group sessions where the planner can meet with operational personnel to discuss the plan, the effects of the plan, and the benefits to be derived from the plan.

Involvement

The last and perhaps most critical implementation strategy is involvement. The involvement of persons and departments affected by the MIS long-range plan should have been ongoing from the first day of the planning effort and continued throughout the implementation. If the planning methodology presented in this book were followed, involvement would be ensured. A poor strategy would be simply to begin implementation independent of the feelings of affected personnel. Failure would almost certainly follow. The implementation process must provide a vehicle for continuous feedback from all involved.

The best strategy is a combination of all four implementation strategies. No one strategy will suffice.

Actual Implementation of the MIS Long-Range Plan

The implementation of the approved MIS long-range plan is the responsibility of the director of MIS. The director cooperates with the corporate officers, user managers, and the ISPC to work toward implementation of the objectives set forth in the MIS long-range plan over the horizon of the plan. The planner functions to develop, not implement. The planner's function during the implementation is to be available for advice and clarification.

The nature of the MIS long-range plan lends itself to the use of a network diagram such as PERT or CPM. Many projects are ongoing concurrently and the completion of some projects is a prerequisite to the initiation of others. To control the implementation, a simple network diagram is recommended. The information in the Project Scheduling Chart, Figure 5-11, can be used as input for preparation of a network diagram.

57. Long-range plans tend to be neglected or, in some cases, purposely overlooked unless a formal periodic review is built into the planning methodology. Progress toward implementation of the MIS long-range plan should be reviewed no more than once per quarter, and no less often than semiannually.

58, 59, 60, 61. It is recommended that three of these four quarterly reports on progress toward the implementation of the MIS long-range plan be verbal, with the fourth accompanied by a formal written report to the chief executive officer and the ISPC. The written report is an annual progress report on the implementation of the MIS long-range plan. The report should list projects completed, started, planned, their status, and the reasons why projects were not completed on schedule (if necessary).

62. An MIS long-range plan may take from six months to two years to develop. The process is continuous after the initial development. The plan can and should be used for performance evaluation. The plan effectiveness, now and in the future, is significantly diminished if it is not used as a benchmark to evaluate performance.

The long-range plan should be completely revised at least once every one and a half years and no more often than once a year. Although the initial document may take up to two years to complete, subsequent revisions of the plan should take no more than six to nine months. If they do, staffing for the MIS long-range planning function should be increased.

The company should establish a policy describing circumstances under which changes to the plan are accepted. Like any production management information system, requirements and conditions of an MIS plan are in a continuous state of flux; therefore, the plan must be updated to accommodate and reflect change. The original MIS long-range plan serves as a framework to which additions, deletions, and changes are made. An MIS long-range plan is a plan of action and should not be altered to accommodate the whims of individuals. On the other hand, the planner must be aware that the plan is not set in concrete. If and when the objectives of a company point in a new direction, it would be ridiculous to try to stick to an outdated' MIS plan. If updates are accepted, they should be critical to corporate operation and kept to an absolute minimum; otherwise, changes will become commonplace, making the plan unmanageable and causing it to lose its validity and goal-oriented direction.

On a year-to-year basis, the maintenance process is very similar to the initial planning process. The same steps and procedures are followed. The obvious difference is that the planner need not start from scratch to develop each segment of the plan. The selling and implementation of the plan become much easier in subsequent years as the merits of MIS long-range planning become apparent.

Part III

Planning Areas

Chapter 7

Policy

ARE POLICIES PART OF
THE MIS LONG-RANGE PLAN?

The MIS long-range planning methodology challenges the information processing management and staff to examine the existing situation and to assess the relative success of information services under the existing policy, operational standards, and procedures. Many organizations operate under implied or generally accepted policies which may not be formally approved or even be in writing. A company can function effectively under such policies as long as no one contests the validity or applicability of a particular policy item. If it is contested, the policy becomes subject to open interpretation, and conflict often ensues. MIS Policy should be in writing and be approved by appropriate bodies [i.e., the high-level MIS steering committee (ISPC) and MIS management staff].

To be successful, the planner and MIS management must be aggressive in their pursuit to establish policy. Personnel, internal and external to MIS, are too often complacent with the existing policy, be it good or bad. This complacency often turns to conflict when an individual is adversely affected by the existing implied or loosely administered policy. Often, the individual turns to alternative interpretations that better suit his or her requirements. In short, a clearly written MIS policy is insurance against many unnecessary internal conflicts.

Conflicts become a part of the planning process when the question of policy establishment is addressed. Therefore, those conflicts that might have been expected at random intervals are concentrated at the beginning of the MIS long-range planning process. It is better to resolve these conflicts at the onset and in a structured manner rather than repeatedly on an ad hoc basis.

JUSTIFICATION FOR MIS POLICY

In every MIS environment, managers and other MIS professionals confront essentially two types of situations: common and unusual. Fortunately, the routine job function deals primarily with common situations. Good MIS policy is directly applicable to common situations and indirectly applicable to unusual situations. Just as good MIS standards manuals do not address exceptional situations, a written policy should not attempt to depict or describe actions or alternatives to all MIS situations. If this were the case, the policy would be cumbersome and difficult to implement. By establishing guidelines for most common situations, an MIS policy will establish a framework by which managers can better cope with exceptional situations. MIS policy need not be comprehensive, but the policy should provide criteria to aid management in resolving exceptional situations.

Many managerial decisions are made by individual criteria. For example, if eight project leaders evaluate and rate the system analyst personnel according to their own approach and standards, fair promotions would be unlikely. In this case, an MIS policy would structure the decision-making process for the good of the individual and the company.

Over the years, the routine operation in most computer centers is crisis-oriented. The manager is forced to make quick decisions before sufficient information can be gathered to support the decision-making process. A good MIS policy will, at a minimum, reduce the potential for managers to make bad decisions.

The absence of MIS policy leaves the door open for people to make their interpretation of what they perceive MIS policy to be. Since MIS personnel work with virtually every facet of corporate operation, conflicts will inevitably arise. Without policy, conflicts can be expected between DP and users, among users, and within MIS.

POLICY AREAS

Personal Information

Depending upon the type of company, data bases will be maintained on company personnel and/or customers. Again, depending upon the type of company, the data base could contain sensitive data and information on individuals. Whenever personal information is maintained, the individuals concerned have an implied right to a certain amount of privacy. Hence, a minimum policy would contain access and disclosure guidelines for personal information.

Personal information should be controlled on a "need to know" basis. In some cases, policy can be explicit as to how the personal data are used (with or without names and identifying numbers, for example).

Policy on disclosure would reference to whom, when, and how often personal information is released within the company and externally. Disclosure policy should consider appropriate state, local, and federal laws.

MIS Charter

Very few corporate computer centers have an explicitly stated charter that details the center's corporate role and responsibilities. Since MIS must be responsible to all segments of the organization, an MIS charter is critical. This is especially true with the recent trend of distributive data processing, wherein roles and responsibilities must be clearly defined. The charter should contain broad statements on goals and/or specific areas for which MIS has responsibility. With the expanded scope of service of MIS and trend to decentralization, user and MIS responsibilities must be delineated. For example, the charter can be used to identify responsibilities for such areas as input/output control, hardware selection and acquisition, data-base integration, telecommunications, office automation and/or word processing, feasibility studies, and application systems development.

When no corporate-approved MIS charter exists, the responsibilities for these areas are often scattered throughout the corporation. For example, the initial phase of input control might reside with the user and another phase with MIS. The result is haphazard control. Another example is the uncontrolled acquisition of minicomputers and word-processing equipment, which can cause serious compatibility and integration problems in the future.

The MIS charter may overlap with established MIS policy but should not contain the level of detail expected in policy directives. The charter should contain a written list and explanation of the charges set forth for the information services department. A typical computer center might be charged with the following responsibilities:

MIS standards, procedures, and policies
Data-base management
Development, ongoing operation, and maintenance of production systems
Maintenance of backup capabilities
Control of accuracy (from source document on)
Physical and logical security
Corporate advisor on issues involving computers and the use of computers
Long-range planning for management information systems and systems integration
User education
Hardware/software evaluation and selection (with input from user)
All physical facilities containing computer equipment (including user facilities)
MIS compliance with federal, state, and local laws
Serve as primary contact for all vendor interaction
Word processing and office automation (and in some cases, process control,

computer-aided design (CAD), and computer-aided manufacturing (CAM)
Serve as catalyst for new systems development

By specifically defining charges for the MIS department, responsibilities for user departments are implied. Although not specifically written into most corporate policy statements (but perhaps a good idea), the following activities are the responsibility of the user in most corporate environments:

Completing source documents (accurately, legibly, and completely)
Data entry (recent trends have been to push data entry to the source)
Completing service requests according to standardized procedures
Informing the data-base administrator of data element and record changes to the data base
Educating MIS personnel in the functional areas
Assisting in the system development process as designated in the methodology
Participating in and evaluating acceptance tests
Periodically reviewing production systems (in cooperation with MIS personnel)
Establishing priorities and other high-level steering committee responsibilities

High-Level MIS Steering Committee*

The high-level MIS steering committee [the Information System Policy Committee (ISPC) in Part II] has been a popular addition to many corporations' organizational structure during the last decade. However, many of these committees were founded without a definite charge. To establish a charge, corporate policymakers must address questions regarding the steering committee's responsibilities, membership, meeting frequency, scope of involvement, and possibly, attendance.
    As an example, the charge of such a committee might include:

Supporting the use of the information services function for an effective and efficient corporate operation. The ISPC should be visible in its encouragement of the information services function.
Presenting a periodic information services progress report and recommendations to the chief executive officer and the board of directors.
Approving or rejecting requests for major MIS services (i.e., requiring more than one person-year of effort and/or a $30,000 expenditure).
Setting priorities among approved information system development projects.
Monitoring the progress of MIS projects and the performance of ongoing

---

*The format of the proposed high-level MIS steering committee is expanded from a format presented in L. Long's *Data Processing Documentation and Procedures Manual* (Reston, Va.: Reston Publishing Co., Inc., 1979), pp. 13-14.

systems using the procedures set forth in existing documentation and procedures manuals.

Arbitrating differences between user departments and/or divisions arising from MIS operations and/or proposed operations.

Setting policy that relates to MIS and affects all departments.

Developing short- and long-range plans for MIS growth.

These are suggested responsibility areas and would vary considerably depending upon the type of industry and committee emphasis. It is implied that the full capabilities of the MIS department are available to the ISPC to assist in carrying out these responsibilities.

The membership of the committee would be established by policy. Six questions need to be answered relative to membership:

1. Who should serve on the committee, and how are they selected?
2. How many should serve on the committee?
3. What is the duration of the appointment of the individual members?
4. Should the director of MIS be a member?
5. Who should be the chairman and how is he or she selected?
6. Should the chairman's position rotate?

The chairman could be elected from among the members or a specific corporate position could be designated as chairman. For example, the director of MIS or the executive assistant to the president are options.

For this committee to be operationally effective, its members should be at the policymaking level, probably vice-presidents. These could be high-level functional area managers and/or other high-level corporate managers. Historically, MIS steering committees, whose members are more than one level of management removed from the chief executive officer, have had little success. Most have, at best, caused no undue hardship and, at worst, been counterproductive. To be workable, the committee must have the power to make decisions, then follow up on these decisions. An MIS steering committee at any level demands that considerable MIS resources be channeled to the support of the committee. Without the authority to act decisively, a lower-level committee tends to operate in circles, thereby wasting valuable MIS resources as well as the time of the members.

Regarding the number of members, experience has shown that when more than eight or nine such individuals serve on an MIS steering committee, the committee becomes sluggish. Too many members make the decision-making process unnecessarily difficult and in general make operation cumbersome. A body of six or seven voting members is recommended. Because most projects of even medium size span more than one year, the appointment should be a minimum of one year with two or more years preferred. Permanent appointments are possible in corporations that have only six to nine potential members. Other more horizontally organized corporations need to rotate this important responsibility. Therefore, a preestablished

appointment period is required. The appointments should rotate in such a manner
that the nucleus of the committee is retained after each appointment period.

To be an effective working body, each voting member must be actively involved
in committee activites. It is therefore recommended that attendance at all meetings be
highly encouraged by the chief executive officer and further encouraged by an
attendance policy. For example, a voting member might be required to maintain a
cumulative attendance record of at least 75% or lose his or her seat on the committee,
and the member and the designated representative must maintain a cumulative
attendance record of at least 90% or lose the seat on the committee. A policy could be
established that automatically appoints a new committee member when an individual's cumulative attendance falls below minimum requirements. The high-level MIS
steering committee should be a committee to which every high-level person with a
special interest would like to belong.

Another policy item would be the frequency of meetings. The committee must
meet often enough to stay abreast of project progress and fulfill other charges set forth
for the committee. MIS utilization is more volatile in some corporations than in
others; therefore, it is recommended that the committee meet no less than once every
two months and no more than once per month. This range of meeting frequencies
has been shown to be effective. Special meetings should be arranged during periods
of high activity.

The MIS steering committee is an arm of the corporation, not the MIS department. The committee should be chartered and given authority by the chief executive
officer. Therefore, this standing committee should report directly to the chief executive officer.

The committee's direct contact with the MIS department should be through the
director of MIS, but the MIS long-range planner would also have continuous and
direct contact with the committee (see Figure 4-2).

User Service Requests

The service request is both the catalyst to MIS activities as well as the undoing of MIS
activities. Policy relative to service requests needs to be clear. Procedures need to be
established to ensure adherence to these policies. For example, who or what body
renders the ultimate decision on whether to implement a particular user request? If a
high-level steering committee exists, it should render decisions on major projects.
Minor maintenance requests should be handled, for expediency purposes, within the
MIS department. The question of policy arises when a designation is required for
what is "minor" and what is "major." As an example, policy might state that the MIS
manager make the decision on projects estimated to require less than one professional
person-year and less than $30,000 expenditure. All other service requests would be
routed to the high-level MIS steering committee (ISPC).

A policy decision should be made on whether to implement an appeal procedure
for users to question a decision not to fund or accomplish a requested service. The
question becomes: Who has the last say? A possible policy is allowing the high-level

steering committee to have the last say. This means that decisions rendered within the MIS department can be appealed to the high-level MIS steering committee.

Another policy statement relative to rejected service requests would be: What should be the elapsed time before the user can resubmit the request for service? If no policy exists, the requestor could break the resistance of the MIS manager or the committee by simply resubmitting the request into the process each time it is rejected. A reasonable elapsed time is four months; however, depending upon the company type, this figure could range from two months to a year.

Policy should be established relative to what information should be included on a service request. Corporations that do not provide guidelines for service requests find comparison between service requests difficult and the information incomplete. Possible contents of a service request include:

Title of the system
A two-alpha-character system identifier (i.e., PR for payroll)
Date of completion of the service request
The names, positions, and affiliations of those who prepared the service request
A general description of the system to include the following: (1) a statement of the objectives of the proposed system; (2) a general word picture of the fundamental operation of the proposed system and the scope of the proposed system, covering all organizational interfaces, volumes and frequencies of activities, complexity of the system, and a gross estimate of personnel requirements
Identification of problem areas in the present system
Justification of how the proposed system will solve present problems: increase services, upgrade management reporting, save money, and so on
Identification of source of funds
Expected date to begin system development, expected implementation date, and any explanation if timing is critical
Identification of all external corporate documents that contain pertinent information
A list of other similar successful systems, including the name of the organization and division heads responsible for the similar system
The general long-range objectives of the proposed system
Other pertinent information

Another policy statement might address the length of the service request. For example, the service request should not exceed seven typewritten double-spaced pages. A total of seven typewritten pages is sufficient to convey the conceptual ideas of even the largest systems. The high-level MIS steering committee will not make a decision to fund a major project based solely on the initial service request. A service request requiring x person-years of effort and/or y dollars of funding would require that a feasibility study be accomplished (x and y being arbitrary). The high-level steering committee would base its ultimate decision on the feasibility study.

After the feasibility study has been commissioned by the high-level steering commitee and accomplished by cooperating users and MIS professionals, the feasibility study is submitted to the high-level MIS steering committee (ISPC) for consideration. Again, a policy needs to be established that identifies action alternatives. A suggested approach is to allow the committee to make one of three decisions:

1. Reject the feasibility study and table the system.
2. Approve the system and assign a top priority to its development and implementation.
3. Approve the system with less-than-top priority and place the request in a queue of other approved systems at an appropriate priority position. Periodically, this queue is reviewed and as resources become available, the committee gives the go-ahead to the highest-priority project(s).

These three points represent one approach to feasibility study evaluation and selection.

Figure 7-1 illustrates one possible procedure for user service request submittal and evaluation.* The figure illustrates the implementation of the example policy statements and procedures discussed in this section.

Personnel Recruiting

Policy relating to recruiting might designate the desired source of future MIS personnel. For example, the existing policy might be to train from within and hire primarily entry-level personnel; or the policy could be to hire experienced personnel to minimize the initial in-house training effort. Recruiting policy could go further and designate minimum educational requirements: a two-year associate degree or a four-year technical degree. The policy could even be more explicit and name curricula (i.e., engineering, computer science, business administration, information systems, etc.)

Other policy relating to recruiting might be whether or not to designate a full-time recruiting staff or to pass the recruiting function around to managers and professionals within the MIS structure. The latter requires close coordination and an ongoing in-house education program in recruiting. This may not be a written policy but a policy that is implied by the MIS organizational structure.

Chargeback System

At some time during the growth pattern of a typical computer center, a policy decision must be made as to whether or not to charge users for professional and/or computing

---

*The user service request procedure previously discussed, and illustrated in Figure 7-1, is part of a standardized system development methodology presented in L. Long's *Data Processing Documentation and Procedures Manual* (Reston, Va.: Reston Publishing Co. Inc., 1979), pp. 20, 22-24.

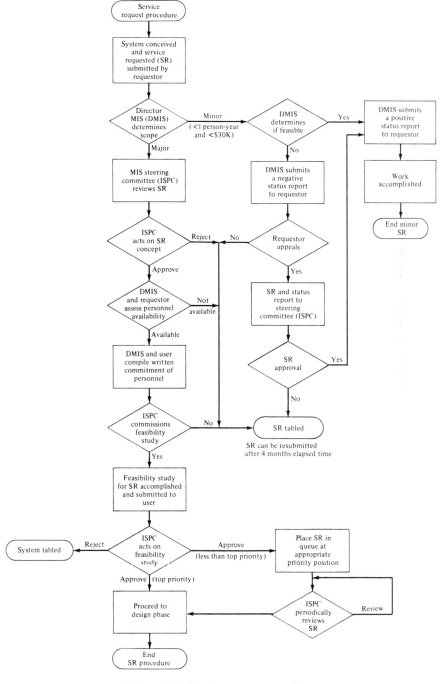

Figure 7-1. *Service request procedure.*

89

services. Chargeback systems provide a vehicle that encourages judicious utilization of these scarce resources. A person or an organizational entity is always more deliberate when spending their money rather than somebody else's.

There are many considerations to implementing a chargeback or cost allocation system. For example, should the user be charged for time and cost of feasibility studies? Should this charge be a fixed amount designated by MIS, or should the charge be based on actual time? Should machine utilization charges be based solely on CPU utilization, or should machine utilization charges be separated for each peripheral device? Should price breaks be given for volume usage?

The chargeback system should be as simple as possible and still provide an equitable allocation of costs. Extremely complex systems add significantly to hardware and software overhead and make internal accounting procedures more difficult. A system does not have to be complex. Use historical utilization data to select appropriate usage parameters. It is possible that one parameter might be highly correlated to overall machine utilization (i.e., wall-clock time), thereby eliminating the need for maintaining complicated and costly utilization statistics.

Hardware Acquisition

The existence of a hardware acquisition policy eliminates the need for corporate and MIS managers to debate the merits of the various acquisition alternatives on the occasion of each major hardware acquisition. Such a policy not only saves personnel time, but adds an ongoing consistency to the process of building and maintaining the hardware base of the computer center. The following is an eye-opening example of what can happen without any hardware policy. One large computer center had twenty-three medium-sized and large mainframes from six different vendors. Another twenty-five vendors were represented throughout the peripheral and support devices. No attempt was made to maintain compatibility between any of the computer systems. The absence of a hardware acquisition policy caused enormous redundancies, blocked attempts at systems integration, created maintenance and accounting nightmares, and made in-house professional education almost impossible. See Chapter 9 for more on hardware acquisition.

A serious problem now facing virtually every medium-sized and large corporation is uncontrolled decentralization. The advent of the inexpensive, full-capability mini-computer has prompted many managers to establish their own small computer centers dedicated to the support of applications in their particular functional area. Decentralization becomes uncontrolled when users are permitted to evaluate and select their own hardware in isolation. Lacking expertise, the user is often sold a bill of goods. To ensure corporate-wide compatibility and the availability of professional expertise, corporate policy should dictate that all hardware acquisition be channeled through a central department, probably the MIS department.

A special case of uncontrolled decentralization is the proliferation of word-processing computers. Autonomous word-processing systems can be simple short-term solutions to one phase of a very complex corporate information-processing problem. Installation of stand-alone, incompatible word-processing systems has a tendency to further embed inefficient and redundant office systems, thereby impeding efforts to integrate corporate systems. Word processing and office automation in general are applications that should be supported by the MIS department. The prudent planner will factor the need for office automation into the MIS plan and press for the establishment of corporate policy to control the acquisition of word-processing equipment.

DISTRIBUTION AND MAINTENANCE OF POLICIES

MIS policy will not be effective if no one knows what the policies are. Therefore, the planner should use mechanisms for ensuring that appropriate personnel know and understand the policies of MIS. One way is to publish a general policy manual that is distributed to basically the same personnel as is the MIS long-range plan. However, this general policy manual should be made available to all persons in the corporation. Certain policies can be stated in other often-read manuals. For example, appropriate policy can be included in operational user's manuals; within MIS, policies can be included in the MIS standards and procedures manual.

The initial MIS long-range plan is the force behind the establishment of MIS policy. However, the plan itself is not appropriate for the maintenance of MIS policy statements. Once policy is established, a separate policy document(s) should be distributed.

Chapter 8

Application Systems

CRITICAL NATURE OF APPLICATION SYSTEMS PLANNING

Each facet of the MIS long-range plan has far-reaching effects on all phases of corporate endeavor, but the driving force and common thread of strategic MIS long-range planning is application systems planning. Therefore, this facet of MIS is perhaps the most critical planning area. Virtually all other facets of the MIS plan are in some way affected by application systems planning.

Most corporations are emphasizing increased productivity as a way to increase profits, but surprisingly, the majority have failed to realize the importance of tapping an existing corporate resource. This resource is information. Every corporation has the potential to obtain this information; however, careful planning and coordination is critical to tapping the information resource. Redundant, autonomous application systems are commonplace and make collection and dissemination of valuable information for managerial decision making difficult, if not impossible. To make the resource of information available, the central theme in application systems planning should be integration.

The application systems planning process will provide insight for a better understanding of corporate operations. The documentation compiled and the knowledge acquired by those involved in the planning effort can provide valuable input to corporate managers whose scope of responsibility spans the gamut of corporate operations.

Important as it is, the application systems portion of the MIS long-range plan is still only part of the plan. Many corporations accomplish application systems planning and call it strategic MIS long-range planning. Such planning efforts are incomplete. Systems planning, when done properly, is completed in concert with other less visible facets of the MIS function.

Figure 8-1 graphically illustrates the activities for application systems planning.

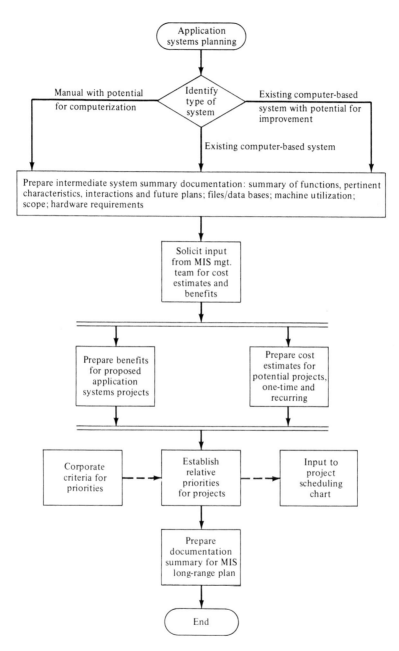

Figure 8-1. *Activities diagram for application systems planning.*

SYSTEMS IDENTIFICATION

The primary purposes of this application systems planning activity are to identify all existing automated systems, manual systems with potential for automation, and existing automated systems with potential for improvement and/or integration with other systems. To do this, the planner must first gather and prepare a documentation package that will give him or her, and others involved, a good understanding of existing systems and those systems proposed for the future. The documentation package that the planner prepares at this time is for intermediate use and should be more comprehensive than the actual application systems descriptions ultimately included in the MIS long-range plan. The following intermediate system summary documentation package should be compiled for each existing manual and proposed system:

> A brief summary that includes a discussion of the basic functions of the system, pertinent characteristics or features of the system, identification of other systems with which this system does or should have an interaction, and finally, any future plans for enhancements or changes to the system
>
> Identification of file types, sizes, and storage media (should be related to an integrated data base when appropriate)
>
> Approximate relative machine utilization, now and over the horizon of the MIS long-range plan
>
> Approximate number of production programs (or relative scope of the present or proposed automated system)
>
> Equipment requirements if equipment is a significant feature (for example, thirty CRTs with tape cassettes)

After the planner has compiled the information, the task of assigning priorities and suggesting areas for integration will be made easier.

The primary input to the documentation of the existing manual and proposed systems is the application system documentation for existing computerized systems, service requests from users, the list of approved projects compiled by the high-level MIS steering committee and the results of periodic system reviews. Unfortunately, the majority of computer centers do not periodically review application systems that they support. This important activity provides management with information concerning the viability, worth, and need for a particular application system. If such a review system is not currently in operation, the planner should initiate the procedure described in the following paragraph to provide valuable input to future planning efforts. Regularly scheduled periodic system reviews are a necessary prerequisite to successful application systems planning.

The System Review Schedule* of Figure 8-2 should be included in the planner's

---

*Taken from L. Long's *Data Processing Documentation and Procedures Manual* (Reston, Va.: Reston Publishing Co. Inc., 1979), pp. 170-171.

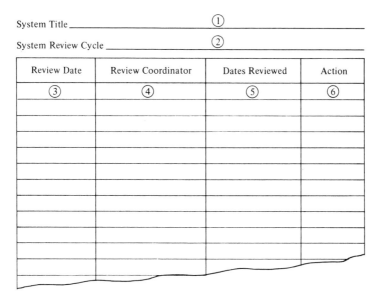

Figure 8-2. System Review Schedule.

arsenal of planning aids. A predetermined schedule completed for periodically reviewing each existing application system encourages both user and MIS personnel to be active in initiating needed system revisions and to be responsive in implementing these revisions. The System Review Schedule is a formal document from which reviews are scheduled, then documented following completion. The circled numbers on the various items of Figure 8-2 cross-reference the following explanations:

1. *System title*: the title of the application system (payroll, general ledge, etc.).
2. *System review cycle*: a set period of time that elapses between reviews (e.g., quarterly, semiannually, etc.). The review cycle should not be less than three months or more than one year.
3. *Review date*: the beginning date of each review. The review dates should be in support of the MIS long-range planning cycle.
4. *Review coordinator*: the name of the person expected to do the review or the person that did the review.
5. *Dates reviewed*: the beginning and ending dates during which the system was reviewed.
6. *Action taken*: Put either "none" or "revised." If the review coordinator recommends that the system be revised in any way, a description of the revisions should be attached to the System Review Schedule. The description should contain appropriate remarks by user and MIS personnel about timeliness, clarity, applicability, format, response time, turnaround time,

procedures, reports, documents, and/or displays. The description would also contain the recommended actions based on the results of the periodic review and the benefits to be derived from these actions.

These periodic system reviews provide valuable ongoing input to the MIS long-range planning process.

COST ESTIMATION

Cost estimates are required for all systems being developed and/or proposed. The cost estimates prior to accomplishing a comprehensive feasiblity study are ballpark figures based primarily on a concept, not a design. Still, the planner should strive to make the best estimates possible. Certain cost information may be available.

For each system in development or for planned development, the planner should make two cost estimates; one for the one-time cost of systems development and implementation, and the other an estimate of recurring cost for production and ongoing maintenance of the system over the life of the system. The latter cost should be an estimate of yearly recurring costs.

See Block 36 of Chapter 5 for a recommended procedure for making estimates of costs.

EXPECTED BENEFITS

An information system, like any other corporate investment opportunity, must be justified. The estimated cost must be paired with the expected benefits (1) to determine if the system should be implemented and (2) to establish a relative priority position. As MIS departments mature, fewer systems are justified solely on tangible benefits. The scope of MIS has transcended basic transaction handling and personnel reduction. Now, through information, systems can also provide insight into the decision-making process. The benefits derived from this type of system are often not reflected in direct or indirect savings in personnel and/or resources.

The long-range planner should list and explain the intangible and tangible benefits of the proposed system. The dollar savings should be associated with tangible benefits, and these total dollar savings (or earnings) should be summarized.

Some corporations have elected to associate dollar savings (or earnings) with certain intangible benefits to prepare a cost/benefit ratio and/or a rate-of-return analysis. In most cases, the dollar figures assigned to the intangible benefits are, at best, wild guesses. Therefore, cost benefit and rate-of-return analysis for systems with many intangible benefits should be tempered with a certain amount of subjective evaluation.

The cost estimates and benefits provide direct input into the preparation of the Project Scheduling Chart (illustrated in Figure 5-9) by providing one-time and recurring cost estimates and information to aid in the establishment of project priorities.

SYSTEM PRIORTIES

Existing and potential application systems must be given a relative priority position for development and implementation. The typical MIS department has a greater demand for services than a capability to supply the services. Therefore, systems must be given a priority.

Each corporation must set its own criteria for the establishment of system priorities. However, the following are criteria for consideration:

The corporate and/or MIS department cash flow would affect cash availability and therefore limit development efforts. However, if resources are available to generate the necesary cash flow, a positive cash flow can be generated by the implementation of certain systems, especially integrated systems.

Another consideration is the interdependencies of the various systems. That is, some priorities are known a priori because one system must be completed and/or designed prior to the development of another; for example, an on-line personnel reporting system may supply the data base for the proposed upgrade to the payroll system.

Of course, the return on investment, cost/benefit ratio, and/or a subjective evaluation of cost versus the tangible and intangible benefits should be considered.

Some systems are obviously consistent with the corporate long-range plan, whereas others' association with the corporate plan is less clear. Perhaps one criterion could be consistency with the corporate long-range plan.

Based on the criteria listed above, the planner should solicit input from MIS management and the MIS steering committee (ISPC). The planner can make recommendations as to which project should be first, which second, and so on. From the input and his or her own judgment, these recommendations should be coordinated with the development of the Project Scheduling Chart. To optimize the use of resources and the Project Scheduling Chart (which includes non-development projects), certain compromises and priority revisions may be required.

SYSTEM DOCUMENTATION

A subset of the previously compiled documentation for each application system should be included in the MIS long-range plan. The documentation that was compiled earlier for the purpose of making cost estimates and setting priorities should be

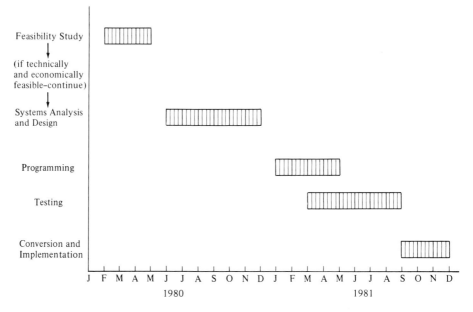

Figure 8-3. *Application systems implementation schedule.*

retained for future reference. Within the text of the MIS long-range plan, each existing and proposed system should have the following documentation:

A brief overview of the proposed project (no more than one or two paragraphs).
Cost estimates with breakdowns into very general categories. (Cost estimate categories should be the same for all systems; see Chapter 22.)
A summary of tangible benefits using dollars as a common denominator and a brief explanation of major intangible benefits.
A proposed priority position relative to other application systems projects.
An optional implementation schedule showing no more detail than the feasibility study, systems analysis and design, programming, testing, and conversion and implementation phases. The implementation schedule can be shown in the form of a Gantt Chart illustrated in Figure 8-3. Such an implementation schedule may be too much detail for medium-sized and large companies.

To illustrate the interaction between the various systems, the planner may include an overview corporate work flow diagram. Such a diagram can be used to illustrate data and work flow interactions between all major systems of the corporation. The diagram should not be limited to computer-based systems because existing manual systems are often prime candidates for computerization and often interact with computer-based systems. The corporate work flow diagram can be used to

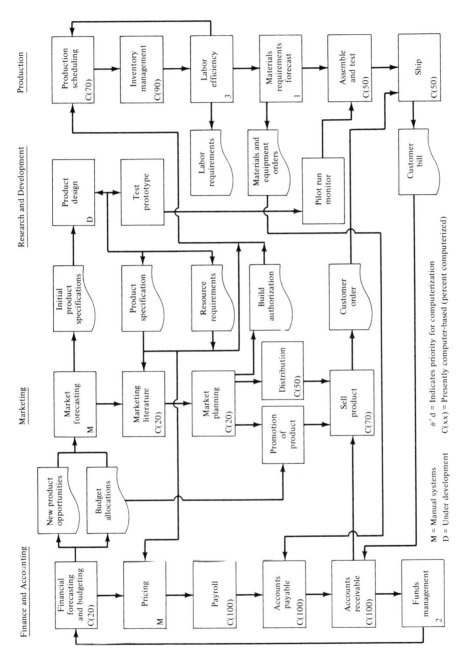

Figure 8-4. *Corporate work flow diagram.*

Finance and Accounting

Marketing

Research and Development

Production

Financial forecasting and budgeting C(20)

Pricing M

Payroll C(100)

Accounts payable C(100)

Accounts receivable C(100)

Funds management 2

New product opportunities

Budget allocations

Market forecasting M

Marketing literature C(20)

Market planning C(20)

Promotion of product

Distribution C(50)

Sell product C(70)

Customer order

Initial product specifications

Product specification

Resource requirements

Build authorization

Product design D

Test prototype

Labor requirements

Materials and equipment orders

Pilot run monitor

Customer bill

Production scheduling C(70)

Inventory management C(90)

Labor efficiency 3

Materials requirements forecast 1

Assemble and test C(50)

Ship C(50)

M = Manual systems
D = Under development

#'d = Indicates priority for computerization
C(xx) = Presently computer-based (percent computerized)

99

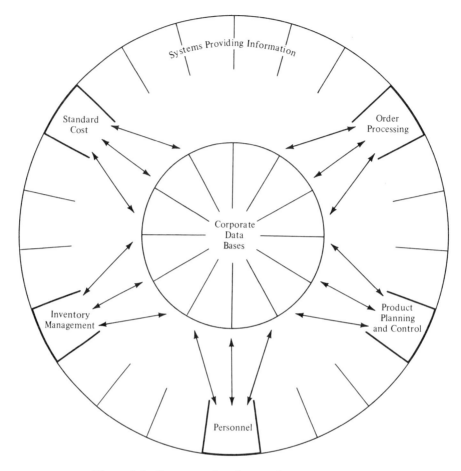

Figure 8-5. *Corporate data base and systems providing information.*

designate manual and computer-based systems, if a system is being developed, if a system is planned for development, or the extent to which a system is computerized. In addition, the priority position for development can be indicated on the chart. Figure 8-4 is an example of a corporate work flow diagram.

The corporate work flow diagram can be compiled in a variety of formats and at varying levels of detail. The purpose of including such a diagram in the text of the MIS long-range plan is to illustrate the fundamental relationships between the operational systems within the company. A more detailed diagram can be compiled later to assist in the implementation of the MIS long-range plan.

Figures 8-5 and 8-6 are supplements, or perhaps even alternatives, to the corporate work flow diagram. As a preliminary step for those corporations planning to implement an integrated corporate data base, the planner would list those depart-

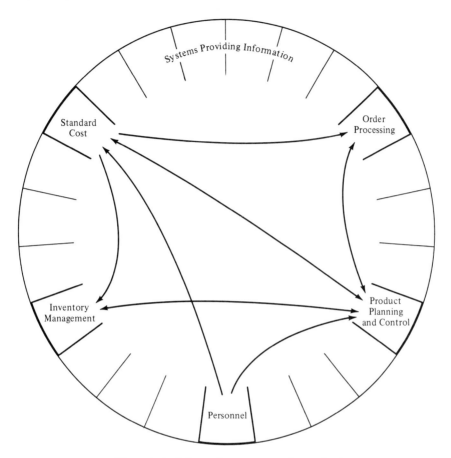

Figure 8-6. *Information sources and uses chart.*

ments and/or functional areas that are data sources or have uses for information derived from the corporate data base. For illustrative purposes, five such areas are noted in Figure 8-5. The planner can graphically illustrate which areas provide data input (are sources of data) to other areas, thereby noting data dependencies (Figure 8-6). Connecting lines with arrows at either end indicate a bilateral transfer of data between areas. Such an overview of data/information flow can be a valuable aid to those project teams working in functional areas, to the data-base administrator, and in establishing priorities for systems development. The MIS long-range planner should coordinate the development of the information sources and uses chart with the data-base administrator.

In summary, the documentation directly related to application systems planning that should be included in the MIS long-range plan is:

1. An overview of each system that includes a description, cost/benefit, recom-

mended relative priority and, perhaps, a suggested implementation schedule for each application system.

2. A corporate work flow diagram that illustrates the relationships between various corporate systems and the computerization status of each.

3. An information sources and uses chart.

This documentation provides a foundation for planning in the other areas that support application systems planning (i.e., hardware, personnel, facilities, etc.).

Chapter 9

Hardware

NEED FOR HARDWARE PLANNING

The sophistication of MIS methods, software, and hardware is increasing at an increasing rate. This is particularly true of computing hardware. Computer systems have become more complex and require periodic upgrades to each of the devices required to configure a computer system. Data communication is playing a greater role in information systems; therefore, the hardware planning traditionally confined to a central facility is now expanded to include communications equipment, communications links, remote computers, and remote input/output devices.

The advent of data communications technology has made possible the implementation of the distributed data processing (DDP) concept, which encourages the decentralization of computing hardware. Decentralization requires a closer control on hardware acquisition in order to maintain compatibility; therefore, short and long-term hardware planning is essential in today's MIS environment.

Impatient users who are searching for complete control are opting to purchase inexpensive minicomputers for specific applications within their organization. Word-processing systems have expanded to the point that they no longer are limited to text editing but encompass the functions of data retrieval and manipulation. Minicomputers and word-processing systems are proliferating in many corporations. This proliferation will inevitably cause compatibility problems and redundancy in the maintenance of the corporate data base. Again, hardware planning is critical to curtail this uncontrolled purchase of computing hardware.

The application systems portion of the MIS long-range plan provides insight into hardware needs. Future hardware upgrades may be directly or indirectly related to the requirements of a particular application system, but application systems planning is the driving force behind hardware planning. When hardware planning precedes application systems planning, systems must be developed to accommodate the available hardware. Unfortunately, this is more the rule than the exception in most computer centers. Systems development is difficult enough without placing unnecessary hardware constraints on the developers.

CONSIDERATIONS

The type and location of computing hardware has a significant effect on everything from organizational structure (centralized versus decentralized), education, and systems integration to the potential for transfer of technology. Even though available information is insufficient to make concrete decisions on hardware acquisition, the MIS long-range plan should reflect a direction and/or emphasis, at a minimum, and some specifics on type and location of hardware. The planner has no control over rapid changes in technology or a knowledge of when a particular device will become economically obsolete, yet changes in technology and obsolescence are key considerations in hardware planning.

In past decades major computer systems announcements by vendors have been predictable within six months to a year. In the recent past and in the future, new computer systems will be announced continuously and the announcements can be expected at random intervals. Although the net effect of continuous new computing equipment announcements is a benefit to the consumer, the planner's job is made more difficult, primarily because of economic obsolescence.

Hardware planning is in essence, the systematic update of corporate computer configurations. The planning process involves the addition and deletion of main frames, modules, and devices, based on support requirements for application systems. The MIS long-range planner should be aware of the following systems configuration considerations:

Compatibility
Processing load (centrally and at remote sites)
Mass storage requirements (direct access, sequential)
Main memory requirements
Input requirements (mode and volume)
Output requirements
Facilities (location and space)
Usage (one, two, or three shifts)
Future needs and expected rate of growth
Backup computer(s)' availability
Time-of-day requirements for on-line users
Communications link alternatives
Data communication support hardware

Most computer centers maintain hardware utilization statistics. These statistics can be a valuable aid in the hardware planning process. For example, CPU utilization statistics gathered over the last two years might indicate an average annual growth of 14% per year. Also related to the CPU, hourly statistics on percent utilization over the 24-hour period of a day can be very helpful. No computer can operate effectively at 100% capacity. Preventive maintenance, downtime, and reruns are a fact of life and must be accounted for when acquiring new systems.

Input/output (I/O) analysis of various peripheral devices and an examination of the available storage capacity on mass storage medium can give the planner insight into the need for peripheral hardware devices.

PROJECTED HARDWARE REQUIREMENTS

Because some hardware devices, especially recently announced central processors, have long order lead times, the planner should project hardware needs over the horizon of the long-range plan, perhaps five years or more. The planner can use the following general categories to present hardware needs in the MIS long-range plan:

Mainframe and memory (identify the use of each mainframe)
Mass storage devices
Terminals (define specific type)
Communications equipment (that equipment between the I/O terminal and the main processor)
Other peripheral devices (printer, card reader, etc.)
Data entry and reduction equipment
Facilities (machine room, remote sites, immediate and long-term data storage, etc.)
Note: Fortunately, the industry has turned the corner on machine size. Even though computer centers are obtaining more and more computing power and requiring more secondary storage space, a machine room of fixed size is accommodating this growth in most cases. Smaller computers are much more powerful than their larger predecessors and the increase in density of magnetic storage has enabled the physical space requirements to remain relatively constant.

The planner can use the Hardware Requirements Matrix of Figure 9-1 both as a worksheet and as a display of hardware needs over time. The Hareware Requirements Matrix matches hardware needs for a particular category with the month the hardware will be required. After the first year the entries should probably be of a general nature (i.e., two intelligent CRTs rather than two IIP 2640 video display units). The three columns on the right of the matrix are for indicating the present-day costs, the cost adjusted for inflation or advances in production technology (or what these devices would be expected to cost when purchased), and the cumulative present-day cost. The second column will be helpful for budget planning. All costs in the third column reflect what the computing hardware listed would cost if bought today. This column contains a running cumulative cost with subtotals in December of each year. If the hardware is to be located at other than a main site, the alternative location(s) can be footnoted and cross-referenced to the appropriate matrix entries.

Hardware Yr. / Mo.	Main frame and memory	Disk and mass storage	Tape	Remote terminals and comm. eq.	Other peripheral devices	WP	Facilities	Present cost	Adjusted cost	Cumulative present cost
1980 Jan										
Feb										
Mar	Add 2M to IBM 3032							150K	155K	150K
Apr										
May										
June										
July										
Aug		Add 2 400M Disks						75K	80K	225K
Sept										
Oct										
Nov										
Dec				1 F.E.P.				160K	170K	385K / 385K (1980)
1981 Jan										
Feb										
Mar										
Apr										
May										
June										
July				20 CRT's 4 Controllers				100K	120K	485K
Aug										
Sept										
Oct										
Nov										
Dec										485K / 100K (1981)
1982 Jan										
Feb										
Mar							Remodel Machine rms	250K	310K	735K
Apr	4 MINIS* for DDP							500K	620K	1235K
May										
June										
July										
Aug										
Sept										
Oct										
Nov										
Dec										1235K / 750K (1982)

* One at each warehouse

Figure 9–1. *Hardware Requirements Matrix.*

Note: Depending on corporate policy, the planner may elect to discount the cash flows in the third column for projected hardware acquisitions. However, since the effects of inflation are offset by advances in production technology, and since announcements of technological improvements are so unpredictable, a realistic compromise is to present hardware costs in today's dollars even over the long term.

ACQUISITION POLICY

The planner should be advised of any corporate policy, either implied or real, regarding the acquisition of computing hardware (see Chapter 7). The following list of acquisition policy statements are simplified examples of the variety of policy options adopted by corporations.

Always purchase.
Always lease (to include lease/purchase agreements).
Lease from a third-party vendor.
Do not mix vendors for a particular computer systems configuration.
Always acquire hardware from a particular vendor.
Automatically order new equipment upon announcement (usually reserved as a policy for very large companies).

There are overwhelming advantages to having an established corporate policy for computing hardware acquisitions. For example, the question of buy versus lease will inevitably surface and be debated for virtually every major hardware acquisition. These decision-making efforts could best be channeled to selection of the appropriate device and not the mechanism for payment. For example, a general policy statement on whether to buy or lease and/or under what circumstances to buy or lease would result in a savings of time to the MIS management team and the planner.

At a minimum, the question of buy versus lease should be resolved. Cash flow within the company is typically the determining factor. The purchase option requires a large initial outflow but results in a substantial cash inflow from investment tax credits and accelerated depreciation. Still, the net cash outflow at the onset is substantially more than the lease alternative. The fundamental trade-off of the buy versus lease question is whether or not to risk premature economic obsolescence. The secondary trade-off is whether or not to forfeit the flexibility afforded by short-term leases. These trade-offs point out the basic shortcomings of each option. The corporation electing to lease equipment is usually afforded a number of options. Some companies offer both short-and long-term leases and a lease with an option to purchase.

Note: The long-term lease (six or more years) may be a viable option for the corporation with a short-term cash flow problem. Long-term leases result in a significant reduction in monthly charges. However, today's rapidly changing technology almost guarantees more computing power for the dollar by next year. Only under rare circumstances are long-term leases a wise economic move.

The question of buy versus lease is not always resolved by selecting the least expensive option. Long-term flexibility, immediate cash flow, and other considerations have a direct bearing on the decision to buy or lease.

PITFALLS IN THE SELECTION OF COMPUTING HARDWARE

In hardware selection, there are certain pitfalls that the planner should avoid. Wholesale mixing of vendors can create serious maintenance and operational problems. This is not to say that mixing of vendors should not be considered, but simply that the planner should approach mixing of vendors with caution. Do not believe everything you are told by the vendor or by a user of the vendor's equipment. Vendors are for the most part honest and wish to provide the necessary information for an informed decision. However, the complexity of computers provides a vehicle to distort truths and to make unrealistic comparisons. All vendors exploit these loopholes. Some users are reluctant to speak the truth about a vendor's equipment and/or their support because it reflects directly on them. A user recommendation of a particular vendor's system should be valued but tempered by the fact that egos play a part in all recommendations. Another pitfall is the signing of a long-term contract (six or more years). These contracts are seldom economically justified over the term of the contract.

HARDWARE EVALUATION AND SELECTION METHODOLOGY*

Hardware costs can consume as much as 50% of the MIS budget and from 0.3 to 3% of the total corporate budget. However, a rule of thumb places hardware costs at 20 to 25% of the MIS budget. These figures highlight the significance of having a hardware evaluation and selection methodology that will consistently result in acquisition of the most appropriate computing hardware. A hardware evaluation and selection methodology not only provides input to the planning process, but is a method of implementing the hardware recommendations in the MIS long-range plan. This section presents a proven method for hardware evaluation and selection.

*This methodology is presented in more detail in L. Long's *Data Processing Documentation and Procedures Manual* (Reston, Va.: Reston Publishing Co. Inc., 1979), pp. 205-228.

Hardware Selection Committee

The hardware selection and evaluation process should not be accomplished by an individual. There are too many variables that require a subjective evaluation. A collective evaluation will yield a more reasonable set of alternatives. For this reason, a hardware selection committee made up of computer center personnel and in some cases interested (and technically informed) users. A committee should have a cross section of hardware, systems software, applications software, and operations expertise. Typically, the chairman should be the primary functionary and would be within the MIS department.

An individual or group of persons within the MIS department should be charged with maintaining an ongoing expertise and knowledge of the computing hardware marketplace, even during times of little or no acquisition. Relative timings, capacities, features, and so on play an important role in the hardware evaluation and selection process. Hardware acquisition is ongoing, even in small corporations; therefore, a continuity of knowledge needs to be maintained from one year to the next.

Communication with the Vendor

If done correctly, the vendor should receive at most three documents requesting input into the hardware evaluation and selection process. The request for information (RFI), the request for proposal (RFP), and the follow-up decision statement after selection are the only formal communications with the vendor. The RFI is optional.

Request for Information

The request for information (RFI) is helpful when the corporation is not well informed of the scope and availability of computing hardware. The RFI has a side benefit that is not apparent when initially sent to the vendors. The RFI can be used to identify interested vendors. Those that do not respond or respond in a lukewarm manner can be immediately scratched as potential vendors. The RFI is not meant to be a request for proposal (RFP) and should be so stated in the RFI. The RFI is simply a letter sent to appropriate vendors to canvass the marketplace and determine which suppliers have viable alternatives and/or are willing to compete for the business. The RFI should include a general description of the existing computing environment and the changes in operations and/or technology that prompted the RFI, some historical perspective, the present computer center configuration (if any), a brief statement of the problem, and any constraints or limitations.

Request for Proposal

The request for proposal comprises information and directions for the vendor, standardized forms, and requests for certain data and information. It is the formal request to a vendor for a proposal. It is recommended that the RFPs be distributed in a joint meeting of computer center personnel, users (if part of a selection committee), and competing vendors. During this meeting, the RFP can be explained in detail and vendors can ask questions necessary to clarify any parts of the RFP that are not clear. The joint meeting eliminates the possibility of unknowingly giving an unfair advantage to a vendor.

Unless standardized forms are utilized for responses to RFPs, the hardware evaluation and selection committee will find it difficult to compare various alternatives proposed by vendors. It is to the vendor's advantage to put the requesting company in a situation where they are, in essence, comparing apples to oranges. Cost is not always the bottom line. Some vendors might offer more capacity than another. The use of standardized forms (see Figures 9-2 through 9-5) provide a common denominator for evaluation of the RFPs.

The text of the RFP should include:

A general description of the past and present computing environment
A time-phased definition of the objectives for the proposed hardware acquisition
    and/or upgrade
A description of alternative approaches being considered

Report Title: System Characteristics	Date	Vendor

Feature	Included in bid	Available		Comments
		Date	Cost	

Figure 9-2. System Characteristics form.

Report Title:	Cost Summary							Date		Vendor	

Item	Initial purc./Rent		Year 2		Year 3		Year 4		Year 5		Total	
	Desc.	Cost	Desc.	Cost	Desc.	Cost	Desc.	Cost	Desc.	Cost	Desc.	Cost
Total net cost, with:												

Page ____ / ____

Figure 9-3. Cost summary.

Guidelines for the RFP responses (scope, format, and deadline)

Details of cost presentation (purchase only, lease, lease–purchase, discount rate, depreciation schedules, tax rate, horizon, etc.)

References (companies who can support vendors' claims)

Award procedure

Award criteria

Proposed implementation schedule

New systems requirements

Contact persons within the corporation (the vendor should be restricted as to who can be contacted)

Included after the above introductory material in the RFP are:

Hardware/software vendor questionnaire

System characteristics

Cost summary

Benchmark results

User surveys

Report Title:	Benchmark Results		Date	Vendor	

Job name	Circumstances	CPU time (seconds)	Elapsed time (minutes)	Response time (seconds)		Comments

Page ____ / ____

Figure 9-4. Benchmark Results form.

The System Characteristics form, Figure 9-2, allows the organization an opportunity to list features that are of particular interest to them. It is not a specification sheet, but it is intended to display cost, availability, and any comments regarding these specifically listed features. The vendor's responses can be more easily compared when each addresses specific characteristics.

The cost summary in Figure 9-3 provides a vehicle by which costs can be presented in a standard format for ease of comparison among vendors. The cost can be presented over time if future systems upgrades are proposed.

*Note:*If discounted cost figures are requested, the discount rate should be identified so that all vendors use the same rate.

The Benchmark Results form, Figure 9-4, ensures a standardized presentation of benchmark results. A form of this type is intended for only the most basic types of information; however, it does allow the selection committee a method of easy comparison of benchmark results between vendors.

Evaluation of Responses to the RFP

The evaluation is accomplished by the hardware selection committee. The Proposal Evaluation Worksheet, shown in Figure 9-5, is used to display graphically both

Report Title:	Proposal Evaluation Worksheet		Date	

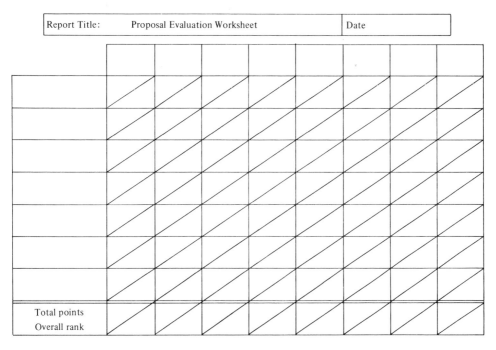

Figure 9-5. *Proposal Evaluation Worksheet.*

individual and cumulative evaluations for each proposal. In this matrix form, each criterion is given a relative point value for evaluating each proposal (100 total points possible). The vendors and/or vendor alternatives are listed on the top of each column. Each criterion, with its associated relative point value, is placed in the respective boxes for each row. Suggested award criteria are total cost, availability of software, system flexibility, system reliability, compatability with existing activities, backup, and an overall evaluation.

Each evaluator rates each proposal against each criterion. The worksheets are gathered from the committee members and the results are tabulated and displayed on a cumulative worksheet. Each proposal can be ranked relative to each criterion and overall. These rankings and relative point values provide valuable insight to the selection process.

These sections of the RFP are discussed briefly below. The Hardware/Software Vendor Questionnaire poses specific questions to the vendor for which you expect a response. This questionnaire should be comprehensive. A vendor wanting the business of a particular corporation will be more than happy to answer these questions. The questions could be on systems software, applications software, communications capabilities, hardware interfaces, environment/power requirements, access controls, reliability, and other areas.

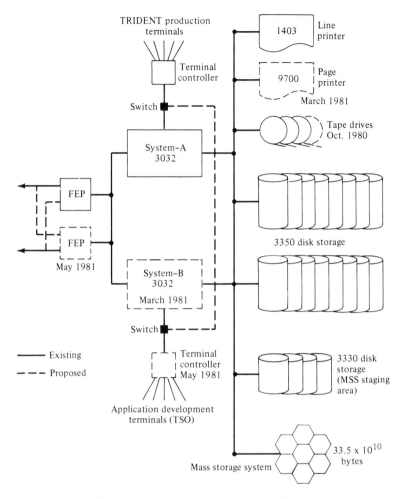

Figure 9-6. Time-phased computer configuration.

GRAPHIC DISPLAY OF COMPUTER SYSTEM CONFIGURATION

Figure 9-6 illustrates how the planner can display both the present (solid lines) and future computer systems configuration (dashed lines) in the MIS long-range plan. Such a configuration chart is helpful not only for planning purposes, but for programmers, analysts, and managers as well. A quick glance at the plan will provide insight into future hardware capacities and capabilities. This is important in application systems analysis and design.

The amount of information that can be placed on the time-phased hardware configuration chart is limited only by the fact that there are limited marginal returns for too much of the information.

Chapter 10

Systems Software

SYSTEMS AND APPLICATIONS SOFTWARE DEPENDENCE

Applications-oriented software (Chapter 8) and systems software are distinctly different in source, concept, and use and are, therefore, presented in separate chapters. Although highly interrelated, these differences dictate a slightly different approach to planning for systems software. This chapter concentrates on planning considerations and approaches specifically for systems software.

Applications software is very dependent on specific systems software products. Systems software is dependent on applications software only in that there is an implied commitment to support applications software with specific systems software products.

SYSTEMS SOFTWARE AND HARDWARE DEPENDENCE

For any given computer, the operating system is often a given. In some cases, several levels of sophistication are available. The planner, in cooperation with technical support personnel, must determine whether to maintain the status quo, take the next logical step, or perhaps convert to the most sophisticated operating system available for that computer.

Users of unique computers or of computers whose manufacturers have only a small percentage of the computer market do not have the luxury of selecting alternative systems software products developed by commercial software houses.

In these cases, most of the systems software is given. The question then becomes whether or not to have a data-base management system, not which data-base management system to use.

The selection of a particular systems software product can have significant effects

115

on CPU overhead and primary storage. In this respect, systems software planning has a direct effect on hardware requirements and, therefore, on hardware planning. By the same token, any hardware change requires an investigation of the possible effects on existing system software products.

TECHNICAL SUPPORT INPUT TO THE PLANNING FUNCTION

An important difference between applications and systems software is that systems software modules are usually, although not always, purchased or are supplied with the hardware. Proprietary applications software is becoming a major force in information systems, but most applications software is still developed in-house. This dependence on available proprietary systems software demands up-to-date input into the MIS long-range planning process. To obtain this input, the planner should establish a formal feedback mechanism (especially within medium-sized and large computer centers) that provides continuous input on the latest announcements and innovations in applicable systems software products. To create this mechanism, MIS management should charge no more than three technical support specialists with the responsibility of staying abreast of available products in their respective fields and with providing feedback to the MIS planner on needed changes and/or how these changes will affect existing and proposed applications software and hardware. The expertise of these specialists should span the systems software categories listed below.

SYSTEMS SOFTWARE CATEGORIES AND CONSIDERATIONS

Systems software can be categorized into several logical areas. These are:

  Operating systems
  Data management
  Language support
  Utilities and performance measurement
  Communications interface
  Management and development tools

By categorizing systems software areas, the planner can develop a standard format for systems software planning which can be more easily updated from year to year.

Operating Systems

Operating systems for any given computer system are usually, but not always, supplied exclusively by the hardware manufacturer. Manufacturers of medium-sized and large mainframes typically offer several types of operating systems to accompany a variety of operating environments (i.e., time sharing, remote job entry, batch processing, networking, etc.).

The general category of operating systems also includes specialized security support packages, software designed to increase throughput, and emulators/ simulators.

Data Management

The primary systems software product in the data management category is the data-base management system (DBMS). However, this category also includes data dictionaries, specialized file organization software, aids to MIS auditing, and software that supports the data entry and reduction function.

The duration of the commitment to a particular DBMS is usually greater than the commitment to other systems software products. The selection of a DBMS significantly affects applications systems design, the corporate data base, and virtually all applications programs. The lack of industry DBMS standardization has almost guaranteed that any DBMS conversion effort will be substantial. More than any other systems software product, this incompatibility tends to lock a computer center into a particular DBMS for at least five years, and usually more. CODASYL has proposed a standard data-base management system structure that is more or less adhered to by several vendors. However, IBM's popular IMS is considerably different and developers of state-of-the-art DBMS's criticize CODASYL's specifications. Therefore, like so many other areas in MIS/computers, standardization for data-base management systems is unlikely in the near future. In summary, the planner must select a DBMS with care, then plan for a substantial conversion effort and a longer useful life than that for most systems software products.

On-line data entry (especially at the source) has been shown to improve productivity and data integrity significantly. Expensive punched cards and key punches are devices of the past and are not presently cost-effective to use or maintain. Any installation would be better served to convert to key-to-disk data entry, whether on-line or off-line. The planner can easily cost-justify such a conversion.

Language Support

The language support category encompasses compilers, interpreters, and other high-level programming systems. Certain programming languages, such as COBOL and RPG, have gained tremendous momentum over the last two decades; but new procedure-oriented languages, and higher-level user-oriented languages are increasing in popularity. The planner has an obligation to at least examine the options. In doing so, the planner should evaluate programmer expertise and preference to assess the potential for new directions in the use of programming languages. In any case, the planner should develop usage statistics on programming languages. These usage statistics, which indicate number of production programs in a given language, frequency of use, and so on, should be collected and evaluated on a yearly basis to detect trends that can be used in future planning.

Interactive program development has been shown in recent years to increase programmer productivity by as much as 100%. The planner in a batch environment would be remiss not to consider this statistic and assess the potential for implementation of interactive programming capabilities.

Query languages are gaining popularity with MIS professionals as demand for one-time reports and on-line inquiry increases, and with users as they take a more active role in information processing. A query language can be oriented to MIS professionals and/or users. If implementation of a query language is to become a proposed activity in the MIS long-range plan, the primary users of the language must be carefully identified. A query language aimed at MIS professionals does not usually pose implementation problems. A query language, strictly oriented to users, demands the attention of the planner. The planner must assess not only the level of user sophistication, but the ultimate receptiveness of users to accept a more active role.

An alternative software solution to meeting a high demand for one-time reports is through the use of high-level report generators. Report generators come in a variety of software formats that include stand-alone programming languages, utilities, and extensions to procedure-oriented languages.

Utilities and Performance Measurement

This category includes all traditional utilities and those systems software products that monitor overall computer systems operations, including job accounting and hardware utilization.

Communications Interface

Corporations that have or are considering distributed data processing (DDP) or the remote linkage of any hardware devices have a vast array of hardware/systems software configurations alternatives. Software support for such configurations can be part of a host mainframe, a front-end processor, a downline processor, and/or an intelligent terminal. Important considerations in the selection of communications interface software are the type of network and actual hardware requirements, corporate philosophy (centralized or decentralized), and the type of application systems to be supported.

Management and Development Tools

This category includes those software products that assist management and the development team in developing and maintaining computer systems. Included are program debugging aids, translators, and a variety of documentation aids. Other software products provide management with information for monitoring and managing development projects. These project management aids are usually based on an established system development methodology.

PRE-SELL SYSTEMS SOFTWARE CHANGES AND UPGRADES

The introduction of a major new systems software product, such as an operating system, will significantly affect job functions of systems analysts, programmers, and technical support personnel. It is human nature to resist change of any kind, but systems software changes and upgrades have created unnecessary hostilities in many MIS departments. For this reason, the planner should pre-sell the need for any recommended changes or upgrades to appropriate MIS professionals before the recommendations become a part of the written MIS long-range plan.

Chapter 11

MIS Structural Organization

Information services is a dynamic corporate function. As applications and computer hardware change, demands are placed on the MIS organization to accommodate new procedures, to develop specialty expertise, and to experiment with other organizational alternatives which better serve the changing needs of the corporation. Organizational planning is discussed in four interrelated areas: staffing, structural organization of the MIS department(s), position descriptions, and MIS committees.

MIS management has the responsibility of making comprehensive, up-to-date position descriptions and a structural organizational chart available to all computer center employees. Poorly designed or nonexistent position descriptions or organizational charts affect morale and cause confusion in the line of authority and responsibilities. In these cases, the organizational structure and position description updates should be included as part of the MIS long-range plan.

STAFFING

Staffing involves estimating and allocating personnel to the various projects and ongoing activities detailed in the MIS long-range plan. The result of this stage of the organizational plan will be the number of persons in the various MIS groups that will be required over the horizon of the long-range plan.

The primary staffing aid is the Requirements Planning Chart for Personnel (see Figure 5-10). Although this chart concentrates on professional development personnel, programmers and systems analysts, the requirements for the support functions (management, operations, and clerical) can be extrapolated using corporate statistics. For example, the ratio of clerical to professional MIS personnel might be 1:7, or the ratio of MIS management to programmer/analyst might be 1:8.

If drastic changes in MIS staffing are expected (increase or decrease of 15 to 20% per year), the planner must pay special attention to the staffing requirements. In effect, an increase would mean that ten extra full-time personnel needed two years hence would probably have to be hired within the next six months. Most new employees complete an orientation and education period of about eighteen months before they become truly productive. In the case of a decrease in personnel requirements, the planner must designate a point in time when a freeze is placed on hiring. In short, the planner should prepare an attrition table.

The planner should keep in mind that any requirements shown in the Requirements Chart for Personnel are in fact net requirements; that is, the planner must consider historical turnover figures and add those expected to leave to those needed to realize the net requirements.

Depending on the size of the organization, the planner can allocate personnel at various levels of detail. For example, for systems development personnel, staff can be allocated for each of the following categories: maintenance, project enhancements, new systems development, and feasibility studies.

The planner should be advised that the potential of an employee is somewhat less than 100% and allocate personnel on the premise that productive time is no more than 75% (the exact percentage would be established by corporate policy, as discussed in Chapter 7). At 75% productivity, four persons would have to be employed to realize three person-years of effort in one year.

STRUCTURAL ORGANIZATION

In organizational planning, the long-range planner's function is to work closely with MIS management and within the limitations of MIS policy and the MIS department charter. They work together to examine critically the present organization and any real or perceived flaws in the organization's ability to serve the corporation. The following aspects of structural organization should be examined:

Line or staff positions
Individual or group titles
Job functions
Span of control
Level of specialization
Chain of command
Committees
Formal and informal communication channels

The purpose of examining the MIS organizational structure is to establish personnel duties and their functional group (i.e., programming) associations, and to establish lines of authority and responsibilities. Often, computer centers do not maintain an up-to-date organizational chart, and in some cases, an organizational chart—period. An effective MIS organizational structure is integral to being responsive to users and is an excellent vehicle to increase productivity. Unfortunately, MIS management is often quick to accept the status quo. For example, in one company the data-base administrator (DBA) was initially aligned with operations. The DBA was totally ineffective in operations, yet MIS management never considered repositioning the DBA function. Management attributed the DBA's ineffectiveness to incompetence. Only after prompting by a consultant did the director of MIS create a staff DBA position. The simple act of repositioning the DBA within the organizational structure solved most of the problems with the DBA function.

The MIS organization is unique in that most corporate entities are more or less autonomous except for their dependence on MIS. On the other hand, the MIS organization must be flexible enough to provide a variety of timely services to virtually every corporate entity; therefore, the organization must be established with an objective to maximize user interaction.

A typical MIS project is an ongoing joint effort with some other organizational entity (a functional area). Very few projects can be coordinated and executed autonomously within the confines of MIS. The MIS organizational uniqueness is highlighted when the technical nature of the function is considered. Relatively few users have a good understanding of computers, the use of computers, and the job functions of MIS professionals, although many have a general awareness. This is paradoxical, in that MIS personnel must work closely with users and assist in accomplishing the basic user job function.

MIS Department Location within the Corporate Hierarchy

The phenomenal growth of MIS in scope of services, budgeted dollars, and personnel has not been reflected in most corporate organizational structures. In many cases the old "DP" function has grown in leaps and bounds, yet the director of MIS still reports to the same position that the original director reported to when IBM 407 accounting machines were used. An MIS department not having a position commensurate with its importance to the corporation is hampered in its ability to provide quality service. This is particularly true when the MIS department does not hold a neutral position within the corporation (e.g., reports to the vice-president of finance).

If the long-range planner and the director of MIS feel that a higher-level corporate position and/or a more neutral position are justified, they should propose alternatives to the chief executive officer and the executive committee. These negotiations and the outcome would become part of the MIS long-range plan.

Decentralization

A recent trend in corporate reorganization of MIS has been to decentralize via distributed data processing (DDP). DDP embodies the advantages of both centralization and decentralization by providing direct service to the user while realizing the advantages of economy of scale. DDP may involve the integration of MIS personnel into the functional areas and, therefore, major changes in corporate organization and

MIS budgeting. Of course, there is no such thing as pure decentralization. A high-level neutral central facility would be necessary to coordinate the following functions:

Hardware evaluation and selection
Establishment of MIS standards, procedures, and documentation policy
Short and long-range MIS planning
Recruiting
Information systems auditing
Maintenance of corporate data base
Establishment of corporate-wide priorities (with help from the high-level MIS
    steering committee)

Conversion to a DDP environment requires not only extensive planning but the solicitation of cooperation throughout the corporation. Details of such a conversion effort would be presented in the corporate MIS long-range plan.

MIS Auditing

Recent federal regulations requiring tighter internal controls, documentation, and continued monitoring of accounting practices have prompted many corporations to form an internal MIS auditing group. To be responsive to federal requirements and internal demands for system integrity, it is highly recommended that an MIS auditing group be created, but not within the MIS organizational structure.

Existing MIS auditing groups have evolved from MIS, internal auditing, or accounting. But now, the effective MIS auditing staff reports to the chief executive officer (CEO). The MIS auditing function is critical to corporate operation and should be given a high priority in the MIS long-range plan. If one does not exist, the MIS planner must work with the director of MIS, the high-level MIS steering committee, and the CEO to fund and staff an MIS auditing group.

The responsibilities of MIS auditing include operational audits (i.e., physical security, procedures for program change documentation, etc.), applications audits to ensure the accuracy and integrity of production systems, and system development audits to ensure that adequate audit controls are embedded in the initial system design.

Reorganization within MIS

The following steps describe a methodology that can be used for reorganizing the corporate MIS function. The MIS long-range planner would work closely with MIS management to document the MIS reorganization set forth by MIS management.

1. Identify organizational considerations.

    A. Assessment of cross section of MIS personnel. The right organization could be staffed with the wrong people, or vice versa.

    B. Existence of paths for career development. The lowest clerical person should have a well-defined career path to the top position. Examine the merit of traditional paths. For example, a programmer does not have to be promoted to a systems analyst.

    C. Whether to distinguish between maintenance and development personnel.

    D. Whether to integrate the programming and systems functions under one manager.

    E. Span of control at various levels.

    F. Need for an assistant director of MIS.

    G. Functional versus geographically organized project teams.

    H. How to reorganize to improve user interaction. Some organizations have established a permanent liaison position. Others periodically rotate functional area managers to work in MIS for up to a year.

2. Identify major MIS operational areas needed to accomplish the objectives set forth in the MIS charter.

    A. Operations
    B. Systems
    C. Programming
    D. Control
    E. Technical support
    F. Administration
    G. Data-base management
    H. Audit (an MIS function but not part of MIS organization)
    I. Career development and education
    J. Data entry
    K. Planning
    L. Liaison function
    M. User systems analysts and advisors
    N. Quality assurance
    O. Standards and procedures
    P. Specialist functions

3. Combine operational areas into organizational groups as appropriate.
4. Identify line and staff relationships.
5. Define job functions and, therefore, positions within each MIS operational area.
6. Supplement formal lines of communication with designated informal lines of communication.
7. Establish standing committees.

POSITION DESCRIPTIONS

Like organizational charts, formal position descriptions are often neglected and become dated. The MIS long-range planning effort presents the opportunity to update MIS position descriptions. Out-of-date position descriptions inevitably cause problems in promotion and compensation; therefore, attention should be given to position descriptions on an ongoing basis, not just on the initial MIS long-range plan. No professional discipline has a more volatile set of career paths. Not only do position requirements and functions change almost yearly, but new MIS career paths are introduced every year.

The planner and MIS management personnel need to cooperate in identifying the items that should be included in each position description as well as the specifics for each item for each position. A possible format* for position descriptions is as follows:

1. *Position title*: Assign a title (maximum of four words) that is roughly descriptive of the duties performed by the person holding that position.
2. *Position code*: a one- to four-character code designating a particular position (e.g., Apprentice Data-Base Administrator—DBA2).
3. *Function*: This segment should discuss in detail the function performed by persons holding this position. List and explain duties in as much detail as possible without limiting the flexibility required of the position. The duties discussions should be very specific at the lower levels and more general as the position responsibility increases.
4. *Responsibility*: List major MIS functional areas and position titles for which the person in the named position is responsible; be comprehensive.

   Note: Certain "functions" may appear under "responsibilities" as well; if so, list in both places.

5. *Interactions*: List and discuss all formal and informal interactions that a person holding the position would have while performing the functions of the position. Do this by listing all titles of persons, both internal and external to the company, who would interact with the person holding the named position. Also, discuss the fundamental reasons for the interaction.
6. *Standing committees*: Name all standing committees, both internal and external to the MIS department, on which the person holding this position would serve and the status on the committee (e.g., chairman, nonvoting, etc.)

   Note: List only those committees or formal groups for which the person of the named position is a permanent or rotating member. Do not list committees for which the person of the named position may be elected or arbitrarily appointed.

*This format was originally presented in L. Long's *Data Processing Documentation and Procedures Manual* (Reston, Va.: Reston Publishing Co., Inc., 1979), pp. 191-192.

7. *Position requirements*: List all minimum educational and experience prerequisites for the position. Also list any desirable education and experience that is over and above the minimum requirements. Label the former set of requirements "minimum" and the latter "desirable."

8. *Salary level (optional)*: Use the standard corporate format for presenting salary data for a particular position.

Note: Since salary levels and ranges are constantly changing, some computer centers may opt to delete this item in the position descriptions and keep these data in a format that is readily available and more easily updated.

MIS COMMITTEES

Committees relating to MIS can be classified in two categories. The first category is corporate committees dealing with the MIS function, such as the high-level MIS steering committee (ISPC). The other classification includes those committees that are established and operate within the MIS department structure. These MIS committees are or two types:

1. *Standing committees*: These committees have a standard set of MIS positions designated to comprise the membership (i.e., director of MIS, systems manager, and operations manager might comprise the grievance committee). These committees usually have regularly scheduled meetings.

2. *Ad hoc committees*: Personnel are appointed to a committee for more intermediate purposes.

MIS committees serve to complement both the MIS organizational structure and the procedures required for the operational aspects of the MIS function. The planner, in cooperation with MIS management, can identify and structure standing committees and also identify the need for various ad hoc committees. These same people, in cooperation with corporate officers, can establish committees which deal with MIS at the corporate level.

The primary corporate committee is the high-level MIS steering committee. The organization of a steering committee would require that policy considerations be made; therefore, the structure and responsibility of such a committee is discussed in Chapter 7.

Possible committees, either standing or ad hoc, within the MIS department are:

1. *Library Committee*: This committee is in charge of stocking and maintaining a professional library of books on all areas of MIS endeavor. The people on this committee would be responsible for monitoring the library budget and ordering those books which are considered good and useful.

2. *Hardware Selection Committee*: The responsibility of this committee encompasses the evaluation and selection of all computing hardware.

3. *Software Selection Committee*: The responsibility of this committee encompasses the evaluation and selection of all software products (systems and applications).

4. *Project Steering and Review Committee*: The members of this committee have the responsibility of monitoring and/or reviewing the progress of major ongoing MIS projects.

   Note: Their function does not encompass the management of these projects. However, such a committee can provide meaningful feedback to project managers.

5. *Grievance Committee*: Within any organization personality conflicts will exist and unwarranted wrongs will be committed against employees. In these cases, grievance committees can be extremely valuable in the arbitration process.

6. *User Committee*: The user committee is set up to encourage a continued positive liaison with users.

7. *MIS Long-Range Planning Committee*: The MIS long-range planning committee might consist of top MIS management personnel and an operative such as a senior systems analyst who doubles as the MIS long-range planner. The purpose of this committee is to provide ongoing feedback on the feasibility and value of ideas and approaches espoused by the MIS long-range planner as well as to render ideas and approaches to the planner.

This list of committees is not meant to be exhaustive, but to provide some insight into what committees might be helpful in the effective operation of a corporate computer center.

In the establishment of a committee, it is important to designate a chairman. A committee without a chairman is usually slow to move. The chairman should be the catalyst in any committee.

ILLUSTRATING THE ORGANIZATIONAL CHART

There are two approaches to illustrating an organizational chart graphically. First, every position can be placed on one (sometimes very large) chart. For large organizations, this can be confusing and difficult to update. Another approach is to maintain a master chart which includes only those individuals reporting to the director of MIS; then subordinate organizational charts are prepared for each division within the MIS department. For extremely large departments, this hierarchical approach can be continued until a reasonable number of positions and/or individuals can be portrayed on one page.

Figure 11-1 illustrates the mechanics of presenting an organizational chart. A line emanating from the bottom of any given position block denotes "line" positions. Staff functions are linked by lines emanating from the side of a given position block. Standing committee membership is denoted by the presence of

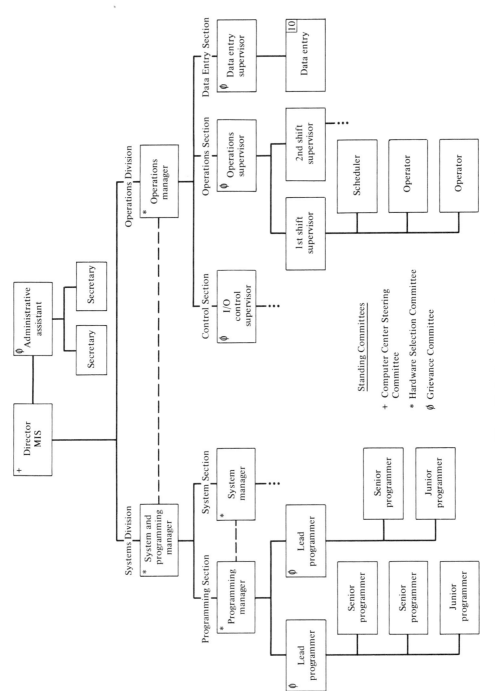

Figure 11-1. Organization chart presentation.

Standing Committees

+ Computer Center Steering Committee
* Hardware Selection Committee
ø Grievance Committee

special characters inside the position blocks. A legend of special characters for standing committees should be included. Solid lines are formal lines of authority, whereas dashed lines illustrate accepted (and encouraged) informal lines of communication. The title of the department, division, group, and so on, is shown above the appropriate manager's position block. The position title and committee assignment(s), if appropriate, are included inside the position block. The number of data-entry operators is shown within a small box in the upper right-hand corner of the position block. When a given position is repeated a number of times, this type of illustration can be used to save space.

The planner can use the proposed organizational chart to illustrate changes over time. This is done in a manner similar to the time-phased computer configuration chart of Figure 9-6.

Chapter 12

Personnel

The variety of problems faced by the MIS manager surpasses that of his or her functional area counterpart. Moreover, the MIS manager is confronted almost daily with demands from every segment of the company. The problems of the MIS manager are intensified by the fact that MIS departments are responsible for maintenance of systems that support the entire company. A user problem is invariably an MIS problem also. Ironically, the most serious problem facing MIS managers is probably the most basic and certainly the most neglected—personnel.

This chapter addresses the personnel problem and is divided into recruiting, retention, morale, education and career development, and salary administration. Although personnel planning may not be recognized as central to planning for information services, successes experienced by information services departments can usually be attributed to the quality, morale, and loyalty of the professional staff.

RECRUITING

In most medium-sized to large MIS facilities, recruiting is an ongoing function, especially in a seller's market. Smaller installations typically hire on an as-needed basis. The recruiting plan is a follow-up to the organization plan and to earlier estimates of staff requirements. The type and level of person required and when they are needed can be determined from these two inputs to the MIS long-range plan.

As mentioned earlier, at some stage in the growth pattern of all MIS departments there is a need to curtail new systems development in order to standardize and formalize internal and external procedures and operations. Although this step may not eliminate the need for personnel, it would affect the type of personnel required; therefore, the planner should factor this possiblity into the personnel planning effort.

There are several approaches to solving an existing or expected personnel shortage. The planner should be advised that recruiting and hiring new people is not the only solution to a shortage of personnel. The wise planner would cooperate with management to at least assess the feasibility of alternative solutions.

Alternatives to Recruiting

Overtime

One option is the judicious use of overtime. MIS personnel consider themselves professionals and are willing to work by the job. It is not efficient to retain a staff capable of handling peak loads within the confines of a 40-hour workweek. This approach results in some persons working at less than 100% during slack periods. Overtime can be used as a buffer for peak periods. Practically speaking, people enjoy working and those not given the opportunity to work full-time lose momentum and motivation. As a result, morale drops in the entire department. Management might consider compensatory time off for overtime work.

Schedule Modification

The Project Scheduling Chart, Figure 5-11, can be used to modify schedules in order to level the ongoing demand for personnel. For example, a two-month project can be expanded to three months, or a one-month project can be slipped forward or backward in time. Any schedule must consider other ongoing projects and the demand on personnel. More often than not, and with little or no sacrifice in meeting MIS objectives, schedules can be modified to achieve a more efficient use of personnel.

Personnel Assignments

Another way to achieve a better use of personnel is through a more judicious assignment of job duties to existing personnel. For example, MIS departments that are organized by functional area teams often have some teams working night and day and others in limbo waiting for another assignment. If existing policy limits the mobility of functional area team members, that policy should be changed to allow the flexibility to assign personnel where they are most needed. Such a change of policy would not only increase personnel utilization, perhaps preclude the need for hiring more personnel, and expand the team members' scope of experience, but would also increase morale.

Increased Productivity

There are many approachs to increasing the productivity of MIS personnel (see Chapter 16). Staff requirements should be assessed only after a concerted effort has been made to increase productivity. For example, the introduction of interactive programming into the environment can increase the productivity of the programming staff from 50 to 100%. The purchase of the equipment and software necessary for interactive programming has a payback of less than one year. This is just one of many approaches to increasing productivity.

Recruiting Strategy

The planner, in cooperation with recruiting personnel, should plan the overall recruiting strategy. In so doing, many questions must be resolved. For example, does the company recruit through commercial personnel agencies, printed media, on-campus college interviews, or do they use a mix of these approaches? Is the in-house education program adequate to enable hiring of inexperienced personnel? The entire process, from the initial candidate contact to the first day on the job, should be meticulously outlined. This is particularly true when the corporate personnel department is responsible for MIS hiring (versus the MIS department) because the variety and scope of MIS positions are seldom understood by the corporate personnel staff. Those corporations that recruit by brute force rather than by planning inevitably pay more for poorer results.

Scheduling on-campus interviews can mean the difference between having success on the college campuses and not having success. Major college campuses fill their interview schedules in the fall very quickly. As a rule of thumb, employers should request an interview date no less than fourteen months prior to their on-campus visit. The company not requesting a schedule may be relegated an interview date late in the spring. By this time the better people are usually considering job offers and are no longer interested in interviewing.

Those college graduates aspiring to a career in MIS can be found in a number of diverse disciplines. The employer simply requesting to interview students in computer science and math (as many employers do) may completely miss their target. Information systems programs are not yet "traditional" and are often found as divisions or areas within established departments in engineering or business. For this reason, campus recruiting visits should be planned well in advance. Order the college catalog and judiciously select the curricula from which you wish to interview students.

Few MIS departments prepare detailed plans for on-site interviews with potential employees. Ironically, a tremendous amount of money is spent in selecting candidates for on-site interviews, but a typical interview scenario would be the following. The candidate is given an itinerary with three to eight names. He or she talks with each one of these people, is asked the same questions, and asks questions to which these people are not able to respond. Because of poor planning, many potential candidates are lost, unnecessarily, during the on-site visit.

The company should coordinate the questions and information dissemination so that interview time is optimized. Each interviewer might be assigned one of the following topics: corporate benefits, career paths, MIS organizational structure, or continuing education. They could also be assigned a general inquiry topic, such as an applicant's academic background, career goals, or technical expertise.

RETENTION

Every computer center in the world has retention problems to some degree or another. A plan to improve the level of retention is in reality a package approach which overlaps other areas of MIS long-range planning. Since retention is paramount to successful MIS departments (also translated "successful corporation"), retention improvement should be an emphasis area for MIS long-range planning.

The retention package suggested by the planner would include everything from total compensation to education to their physical working space. Even programmers, analysts, and MIS managers have a hierarchy of needs. Within any given corporation, the planner must identify these needs and work to prepare a package designed to encourage personnel to remain with the company. The planner would then develop a system and a timetable for implementation of the retention portion of the plan.

MORALE

Once morale is identified as an ongoing problem within the MIS organization, it is encumbent upon the MIS long-range planner to confront the problem in the plan. The planner, in cooperation with management, might recommend that certain steps be taken to improve morale and, therefore, productivity. For example, the implementation of flexible working hours has been a plus in some companies. Many facets of the MIS long-range plan have a direct effect on morale: education, organizational structure, position descriptions, career path development, and others.

EDUCATION AND CAREER DEVELOPMENT

The dynamic nature of the computer industry places demands on MIS management to maintain an up-to-date and high level of expertise in the various career fields within MIS. To do this, management should provide a comprehensive continuing education program for every person in an information services career path. The education program serves three major purposes: to keep personnel at the state of the art, to provide an environment that is proactive rather than reactive, and to provide a formal vehicle for career development.

Each employee should know what is required or expected in order to move from one job position to another. Career paths should be well defined and in writing. The mere establishment of a career development program will have a positive effect on morale.

In companies where a comprehensive education and/or career development program does not exist, the planner should consider recommending that someone be appointed as an education coordinator. Such an action would affect the organizational plan. An education program is established by MIS management via a matching process that matches MIS department objectives with the required education for each position type.

The education coordinator is the key to implementation of an education program. The coordinator functions to:

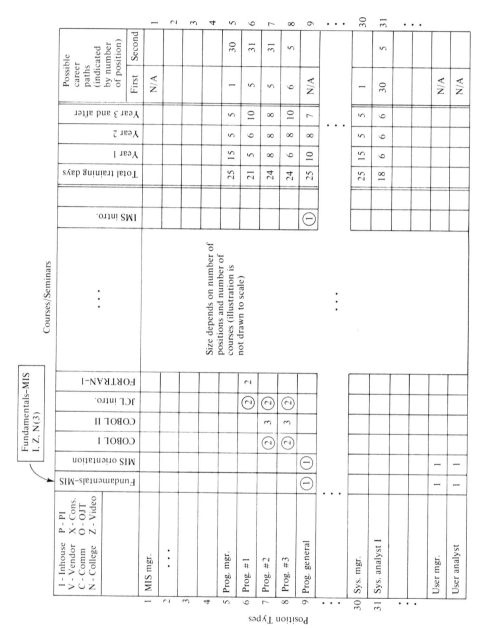

Figure 12-1. *Education and Career Development Matrix.*

Coordinate all MIS education.

Maintain education records on all MIS personnel.

Maintain files on available courses (content and accumulated critiques).

Plan and coordinate all in-house education programs.

Select and provide education programs for in-house instructors.

Schedule MIS personnel in courses and seminars.

Administer the MIS education budget.

Assist MIS management in counseling personnel in career development.

The education and career development matrix* shown in Figure 12-1 is a vehicle by which the entire education program can be constructed, graphically illustrated, then monitored. Essentially, the matrix indicates which courses are required, over time, for personnel in a particular position type (i.e., programmer 1). Also noted are the sources and durations of each course. The blowup of the first course entry in Figure 12-1 indicates that the "Fundamentals—MIS" course can be found as an in-house offering (I), on video cassettes (Z), and in local colleges (N). The "3" indicates that the average course duration is approximately three working days.

Some consider user education to be the key to successful MIS operation. Any plan for in-house MIS professional education should also include education for users. This education would be of two types: general MIS education for user management and analyst, and education relating to the operation of a given system. Any education program for MIS professionals should be expanded to accommodate user education.

In planning for education and career development, the planner might recommend that a company-wide skills inventory be developed as a by-product of these programs.

SALARY ADMINISTRATION

At least one person in information services should be in touch with the local and national market for MIS professionals. The MIS long-range planner is usually assigned this responsibility. The planning phase of salary administration plays an important role in establishing salary objectives for various levels of personnel and for developing the plan for merit-based salary increases. It is bad for morale and professional growth to set salaries based on a manager's whims versus a rigorous methodology of salary administration. If such a methodology does not exist, the planner should consider this a high priority in his or her list of planned projects.

The planner should recognize that, because of the mobility of MIS professionals, there is a fine line between setting salaries below scale and at or above the market.

---

*The details for compiling the Education and Career Development Matrix are found in another book by L. Long, *Data Processing Documentation and Procedures Manual* (Reston, Va.: Reston Publishing Co., Inc., 1979), pp. 195-201.

Those companies providing a compensation package that is slightly below the local norm will inevitably experience a higher turnover rate. The irony is that the constant hiring and educating of people to replace those that leave may require as much as five times the expenditure required to raise the salary level to local norms. Planners should bear this in mind.

Chapter 13

Management

Since the first commercial computer was installed in the U.S. Census Bureau, MIS professionals have been more adept at solving technical rather than managerial problems. The lack of managerial expertise and/or interest still exists, but to a lesser extent. However, management of the MIS function is still one of the most pressing problems facing MIS. Over the last decade there has been a significant shortage of MIS professionals, and the shortage is even more acute for MIS managers. The lack of capable managers and the unwillingness of primarily technical people to accomplish the management function are only part of the MIS management problem.

Many MIS managers use the seat-of-the-pants approach to management. Management, like programming, requires highly developed skills and use of the latest technology to be effective. Tools supporting the programming function may be more highly developed than those supporting the management function, but management tools have been developed that are a significant aid to management of the MIS function and should not be overlooked in the planning process. These management tools can be likened to applications systems in that the implementation of each would be considered a project: analysis, design, implementation, and evaluation. For this reason, the planner should not only evaluate the state of the art of MIS management within the corporation, but make recommendations for improving management expertise and techniques.

MIS MANAGEMENT SYSTEMS

Those aspects of MIS management that overlap the planning process and are not discussed more appropriately in other chapters of this book are discussed here. The planner would work with the director of information services to identify what tools, techniques, procedures, or principles should be evaluated and, perhaps, implemented.

MIS Management Matrix

A major premise of the MIS management matrix (MMM) is that the areas of MIS (e.g., performance evaluation, planning. hardware acquisition, etc.) are highly interrelated. It is encumbent on MIS managers to identify how each area is related to the other areas. The MIS long-range planner, in the course of accomplishing the planning function, will have a major input in this task.

The MMM approach assumes that a manager can learn and understand the various areas of MIS operation, then use an MMM to identify considerations and tools needed to solve a particular problem or to address a particular area of MIS. The matrix, as the name implies, provides a cross-reference between the designated areas of MIS. The areas would be listed alphabetically along the left-hand side and at the top of the matrix. The manager would identify possible categories of relationships between any two areas. For example, an area listed at the top would be matched with a left-hand-side area as one of the following:

1. A management consideration or a source of input.
2. A tool, and one that should be integrated with the left-hand-side area.
3. Both of the above.

These categories are listed merely as examples. The MIS manager would select categories best suited to render a clear picture of the relationships of the various areas within MIS. The optimum level of detail would vary considerably among corporations, depending on size. The areas listed below could be combined and summarized for smaller corporations (ten to thirty areas). The MIS planning process in larger corporations requires a greater attention to detail (thirty to seventy-five areas). The following are possible matrix entries and should prove helpful in the preparation of an MMM.

Application Systems (MIS)	Conversion
Audit	Cost/Benefit Analysis
Benchmarks	Data-Base Management
Budget Preparation	Data Communication and Network Configuration
Career Development Programs	Data Reduction and Integrity
Certification and Professionalism	Distributed Data Processing
Chargeback Systems and Cost Allocation	Documentation
Committees	Estimation
Communication (Verbal and Written)	Evaluation and Ongoing Operation
Consultants	Facilities Planning
Contingency Planning	Feasibility Studies
Contract Systems Development	Goals Setting
	Growth

Hardware Evaluation and Selection
Image (PR)
Implementation
Legal Implications and Federal Regulations
Library (MIS)
Maintenance and Reliability of Hardware
Maintenance of Software
Management by Objectives (MBO)
Manuals and Directives
Models
Morale and Motivation
Office Automation
Operations (Machine Room and Controls)
Organizational Structure
Performance Measurement and Personnel Evaluation
Periodic System Reviews
Planning
Policies
Political Arena
Position Descriptions
Priority Establishment
Privacy

Procedures
Productivity
Programming
Project Management and Control
Proprietary Software
Quality Assurance
Recruiting, Retention, and Termination
Roles and Responsibilities (DP and User)
Salary Administration and Compensation
Security (Logical and Physical)
Social Impact
Software Evaluation and Selection
Staffing
Standardization
Structured Approaches and Methods
Systems Analysis and Design
Systems Development Process
Technology Transfer
Top and User Management Interactions
Training/Education Programs
User Seminars
Vendor Relations and Contracts
Word Processing
Working Hours

The MIS management matrix is not only an excellent tool for MIS management, but can provide valuable input into the MIS long-range planning function. MMM is not to be confused with the concept of "matrix management." Where matrix management is oriented primarily to personnel and organization, the MIS management matrix deals with interactions between the areas of MIS.

Project Management and Control

Project management and control has been a continuing problem in the MIS environment because of the lack of standardized system development methodologies on which to base such a system. A good project management system will provide management with the information to make reasonable estimates and to get the job done on time and within budget. Without some type of system to provide management with ongoing project status information, management cannot adequately follow the progress of a particular project, much less a number of parallel projects.

Once a workable systems development methodology has been implemented, a project management and control system can be implemented easily. Both are prerequisites to a successful MIS environment.

Performance Evaluation

Performance evaluation is a "system" that encompasses a range of activities from manager-subordinate contracts and periodic performance reviews to termination of an employee. The system includes the production of a written contract that is agreeable to both the manager and the subordinate, possibly using the MBO (management by objectives) technique. Personnel at various levels in the MIS organization are rated during periodic performance reviews. A written report of the evaluation, critical for both promotion and termination, is produced after each review session.

The absence of a performance evaluation system renders management unprepared to delineate top performers from mediocre performers. This affects morale and the overall effectiveness of the MIS department.

Modeling

Used judiciously, modeling techniques can provide valuable information to enhance the decision-making process for MIS managers. Models can be used to forecast trends, simualte on-line systems, schedule projects, and make estimates. Most models, once developed , require an extensive data base from which to extrapolate trends, simulate an activity, or make estimates. Several years of data collection may be necessary before a model can be used. For example, comprehensive historical data are necessary to make accurate project estimates of time and personnel requirements. The planner must get involved early to lay the foundation for the use of models.

Management Reporting

Information services, like any other functional area, benefits from information that aids in the decision-making process. Certain computer-based information systems should be designed and implemented to support MIS decision making. The planner should establish planning objectives to achieve the following minimum reporting requirements:

> Budget (actual versus budgeted expenses)
> Overtime and exceptional cost reporting
> Hardware utilization (by device)
> > Wall clock
> > Actual usage time

Staffing reports
    Current versus authorized staffing
    Ongoing efforts to meet minimum staffing levels
Utilization of personnel (by section)
Turnover (by section, by reason left)
    Dissatisfied
    Terminated
    For promotion
Equipment status
    Mean time before failure (MTBF)
    Mean time to repair (MTTR)
On order and installation plans
Project management
    Ahead/behind status
    Costs

These MIS management reporting areas would be considered a minimum for successful MIS departments.

Chapter 14

Operations

The operations section of most MIS departments operates the hardware and runs production systems selected and/or developed by sister MIS functions. The purpose of operations is to take these "givens," hardware and software, and schedule production to meet designated deadlines. The MIS long-range planner becomes involved in operations planning primarily in the areas of staffing and general scheduling.

STAFFING CONSIDERATIONS

Since the number of working hours affects the amount of hardware required, the planner would be involved in policy decisions on whether operations personnel work one, two, or three shifts and/or which days have how many shifts. A few corporations have elected to purchase large computer systems that can handle the vast majority of the work during a day shift. This, of course, is a costly approach to providing information services (but is necessary in some cases).

Multiple shifts are almost a prerequisite to a good security policy. The planner should ensure that operators are regularly rotated between shifts so that one operator is not solely responsible for running a particular production system over an extended period of time. A great many computer centers today violate this very important security precaution. A knowledgeable operator with sole responsibility for a given production system creates the potential for disaster.

Another security concept that overlaps with staffing is segregation of duties. Planning for segregation of duties begins during the systems development process. Systems design efforts should follow the dictates of segregation of duties, which emphasize that data preparation, processing, and output validation (control) be accomplished by separate groups.

The planner is the person primarily responsible for estimating personnel requirements for the entire data center, including operations. To do this he or she must work closely with the operations manager to ensure that personnel are available and qualified to use the equipment in the most efficient manner. Unfortunately, under-staffing in operations is widespread. The last place any computer center should look to save dollars in labor costs is in the machine room. The following example is real and illustrates why. A computer center elected to operate a $300/hour computer with one $7/hour employee. The result was a 50% machine utilization. The addition of another operator at $7/hour would provide access to $150 (.5 × $300) worth of machine time not available with one operator. The computer center saved $7 per hour by not hiring a second operator. When medium-sized to large computers utilization by not hiring a second operator. When medium-sized to large computers cost anywhere from $50 to thousands of dollars per hour, a small inefficiency in machine room operation can result in substantial losses to the company

SCHEDULING

Application systems should be scheduled to utilize equipment in an optimum manner while meeting production deadlines. Many computer centers are utilizing automated scheduling packages provided both by vendors and commercial software houses in order to set up the job stream based on programming dependencies and frequencies. These automated packages not only minimize operator intervention, but minimize the possibility of human error in initiating a particular job stream. These systems provide for applications scheduling, monitoring of systems status, and report generation.

Computers, like other mechanical devices, require periodic maintenance. Certainly, the most efficient approach to maintenance is preventive maintenance. Like application systems, preventive maintenance must also be scheduled. The Operations Work Chart, Figure 14-1, shows how applications systems can be planned with preventive maintenance. A work chart could be prepared for each day of the week, showing standard daily production systems. Similar charts could be prepared for week-end, month-end, quarterly, and/or yearly deviations from normal daily operations.

The Operations Work Chart can be used as an aid in scheduling not only production systems and preventive maintenance, but other machine-dependent activities. Other activities include:

Program development and testing
System quality assurance testing
Data and file conversion
Live testing (prior to parallel operations)
One-time and/or ad hoc jobs
General maintenance
Hardware upgrades or additions

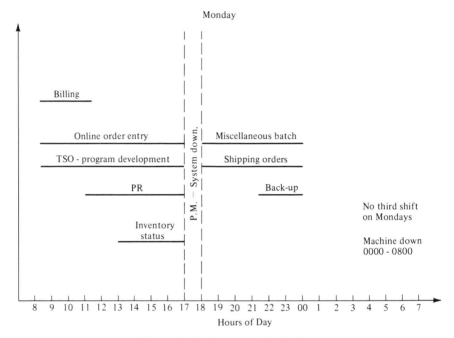

Figure 14-1. *Operations Work Chart.*

From the list above it is apparent that the planner must work closely with the operations manager in planning for hardware upgrades, system conversion, and implementation.

Chapter 15

Standardization of Documentation and Procedures

Companies considering or engaged in the process of comprehensive MIS long-range planning for the first time should accompany this activity with standardization of documentation and procedures (if they do not exist). Historically, these functions are formally initiated at approximately the same point in a typical computer center growth pattern.

For the purpose of this discussion, standards, documentation, and procedures are defined. A reference to standards depicts a specific (standardized) approach or way to do something that is applicable to all concerned. Documentation is that written material which graphically and verbally depicts a system, a process, or a procedure (e.g., systems and programming documentation, user's manual, hardware / software selection process, MIS long-range plan, etc.). Procedures refer to a way of accomplishing something and includes defining tasks and responsibilities. The relationship among the three terms is sometimes misinterpreted. An MIS standard procedure refers to a procedure that is applicable to all concerned. Documentation is the intermediate and permanent written material that results from MIS personnel and users following standard procedures.

People often refer to standardized procedures and standardized documentation. For the purpose of discussion they can be addressed separately, but, in reality, one is of little value without the other. Procedures without the accompanying documentation or documentation without procedures by which to compile it render both unmanageable and often useless.

STANDARDIZATION CYCLE

Figure 15-1 illustrates the relationship among standardized procedures (methodologies), technical methods, management, and documentation. Given a methodology that includes technical methods with accompanying procedures, documentation

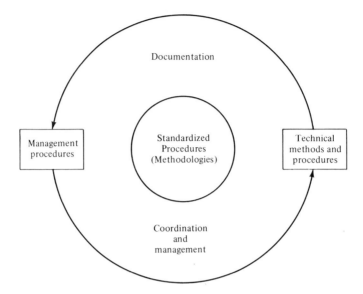

Figure 15-1. *Standardization cycle.*

provides management with the capability to review, via documentation, whether the project is meeting objectives and/or an acceptable level of quality. Through documentation, management also has the capability to monitor project progress. This documentation provides a framework by which management can coordinate and control what takes place within the structure of the standard procedures; thus, the cycle is complete.

PROCEDURES

The bottom line in the MIS environment is "procedures." Unfortunately there has been an overemphasis on the micro-level segment of systems development and operation and, consequently, components of the system are addressed independently of each other. Procedures are necessary to integrate the various components of both system development and operation.

The planner should identify areas in which procedures should be developed and/or improved. Each procedural deficiency should be thought of as a project and given the same level of emphasis as a computer systems project. The planner might assess the need for establishing (or revising) procedures on:

> Systems service requests
> Employee performance evaluation and merit salary administration (integrate with career development)

Application system reviews
System development methodology
Preventive maintence for hardware
Grievance
Appeals (for rejected proposals)
MIS long-range planning

The planner should also investigate the need for revising major corporate procedures which place unnecessary constraints on the development or operation of application systems. For example, some corporate guidelines become outdated and limit the potential for the information system to be effective and responsive.

In all probability, the planner will be involved directly in the definition of certain standardized procedures. An important point to remember is that procedures are applicable to all concerned and they must be readily understood and not subject to interpretation. Any standardized procedure should be developed, worked, then reworked, until it is in its most basic format.

DOCUMENTATION

Surprisingly, few computer centers have standardized documentation. Of those that do, few have the accompanying procedures necessary to ensure proper and timely completion of the documentation. Within the text of the MIS long-range plan, it may be advisable for the planner to accompany a recommendation with cost justification for developing stanardized procedures and documentation. This justification is often necessary input to convince top management that procedures must be followed and that documentation must be completed according to those procedures. The occasional "I-want-it-yesterday" syndrome displayed by top management can serve to deter adherence to standardized procedures.

Examination of the total cost of a computer-based information system over the life of the system supports the premise that the development cost is just the tip of the iceberg, yet development cost is given the most attention. Figure 15-2 illustrates that, although cost may be high initially, ongoing production and maintenance costs of well-documented and conceived information systems will be much less over the life of the system. By following a standardized procedure (system development methodology), the probability is much greater that the system will be what the user requested and, therefore, more responsive on an ongoing basis. Historically, good information systems require less maintenance, and maintenance is easier when support documentation is up to date and available.

Major documentation decisions must be made during the planning process. To illustrate, assume that a system development methodology is adopted. The planner must work with the systems group to identify existing application systems that need to be updated to accommodate the proposed systems development methodology. Some re-documentation efforts would be considered a major project. This decision

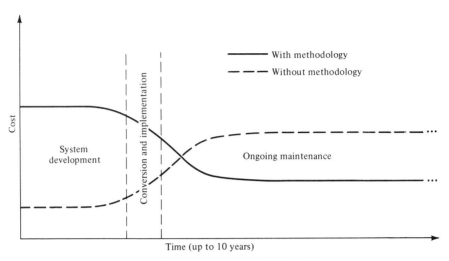

Figure 15-2. *System cost over the life of the system.*

is usually made on a purely economic basis. Each computer system has a life cycle. If the system is near the end of the life cycle, is it justified to devote time to update the documentation to the new format? In all probability, some systems should remain operational with the documentation unchanged. The planner would also be involved in the decision to rework certain systems currently under development in order to accommodate the new methodology. This decision would involve an assessment of the flexibility of the proposed project deadlines.

MIS MANUALS AND/OR DIRECTIVES

MIS standardized procedures and documentation practices are usually distributed and circulated in the form of an internal MIS manual and/or directive. Standardized procedures have little impact on the information services function if they are not put in writing and made available to those who might use them. Therefore, the planner should not only identify existing manuals and directives, but assess their quality, availability, and utility

Expertise in developing internal MIS manuals and directives is limited. Each year thousands of manuals are developed, but only a small percentage are useful and fully implemented. There are several reasons why this is so. Manual content is often developed to consider virtually all possible circumstances, thereby making it too voluminous for easy reference. Still, most are too general in their explanations of "how to do it" and "what to do." Activities described are not interrelated or sequenced. Many directives and manuals promote user interaction, yet are designed by and for MIS personnel without regard for the total audience (this includes users).

More often than not, the development of an MIS manual is an assignment that is peripheral to an individual's primary job function; consequently, they are not given sufficient time or motivation to produce a high-quality product. The average computer center will have a number of manuals and directives that are in theory applicable, but in fact have not been followed for years. The planner should move to discard or revise these manuals or directives.

The planner can use the following list of possible MIS manuals and directives as a check list to determine whether such a manual or directive exists or should exist, and whether it is up to date and applicable.

> User manuals for the various production systems
> MIS audit checklist
> Budget preparation process
> Education and career development program
> Structural organization—organizational chart, position descriptions, and committee descriptions and charges
> Statement on acceptable levels for verbal and written communication
> Systems development methodology, including standardized procedures and documentation
> Programming conventions
> Hardware evaluation and selection procedure
> Software evaluation and selection procedure
> Word-processing and minicomputer acquisition procedures
> Applicable federal regulations
> Management by objectives (MBO) process, if applicable
> Personnel performance measurement and evaluation system
> MIS long-range planning methodology
> MIS long-range plan
> MIS policy
> Project management and control system
> Recruiting procedures
> Salary administration and compensation
> Security and risk analysis procedures
> Disaster or contingency plan

This list, although not exhaustive, includes most areas in MIS that should be supported by a written document. Some computer centers will combine list items into one manual or directive.

Chapter 16

Productivity Improvement

Management is often too willing to accept the status quo. User demands, ongoing maintenance of production systems, and other pressing items cause management to overlook planning for the obvious—productivity improvement. MIS management must take direct action to improve productivity, and these actions must be carefully planned and included in the MIS long-range plan. To assess improvements in productivity, MIS management must be prepared to measure and evaluate their efforts.

The MIS long-range plan is not only a vehicle but a catalyst for productivity planning. Many facets of the plan can be manipulated to create the environment for increased productivity. The planner should emphasize the various facets in which there is a potential for increased productivity and suggest methods and approaches for productivity improvement.

POSSIBLE APPROACHS TO INCREASED PRODUCTIVITY

The following list of possible approaches to increasing productivity is not meant to be exhaustive. The list is intended to present the planner with several strategies that others have found successful.

Use of Standardized Methodology

The economics of and justification for implementing a standardized systems development methodology were discussed in Chapter 15. Methodologies have a positive effect on personnel productivity. For example, ultimately the use of a standardized methodology will change the ratio of maintenance to new systems development work. A standardized methodology ensures a higher-quality system and, therefore, minimizes the ongoing maintenance. Any decrease in maintenance provides a net increase in personnel available for new systems development, thereby increasing productivity.

More Responsive Structural Organization

Organizational planning was discussed in detail in Chapter 11.

Maintaining a Comprehensive Education and Career Development Program

An MIS department does not always have the in-house expertise to respond to a user's request. Consequently, they react, go through the education process, then address the user's needs. An ongoing education program that anticipates user needs could minimize unnecessary delays in responding to these needs. See Chapter 12 for details.

Implementation of Interactive Program Development

Computer centers have experienced from 50 to 100% increases in programmer productivity by converting from batch to interactive program development.

Collection of Data at the Source

By collecting data as close to the source as possible, the number of times a transaction has to be transcribed is minimized and accuracy is increased. Many companies have users complete a hard copy and physically deliver it to on-line operators within the computer center who transcribe the data to a machine-readable format. In most environments, data entry can be done more accurately and more efficiently by the user, thereby eliminating at least one step in the transcription process.

Use of High-Level User-Oriented Languages

Attention by MIS professionals to one-time user requests for special reports is minimized with the existence of a high-level user-oriented language. With proper education, users can obtain their own one-time reports.

Use of a Data-Base Management System

Data-base management systems provide an environment for systems integration and, therefore, efficient programming. They also provide information not readily available using traditional flat files.

Physical Facilities

It has been shown by human factors engineers that the design of a work space has a significant effect on the productivity of the worker. Simple attention to office space and arrangement of the work space may result in substantial increases in productivity.

Attention to other physical facilities, such as the machine room and its arrangement, terminal rooms for programmers, and I/O distribution centers, can also affect productivity.

Attention to Personnel

A particular hiring policy may improve the potential to hire personnel with substantially greater capability to produce than other potential employees. In addition, attention to motivation through incentives, bonuses, education career development, title, job functions, and so on, will ultimately affect productivity.

Project Management

The MIS long-range planner can take this opportunity to recommend project management procedures for control, scheduling, performance evaluation, and allocation of resources for projects. Integration of existing or proposed methodologies with a project management technique can improve productivity significantly. The MIS environment is project oriented by nature; therefore, it behooves each MIS manager to accommodate this idiosyncrasy by implementing a project management system. The planner should consider this when recommending methodologies and other management techniques.

Application Systems

Each application system has a set of procedures that may or may not result in the most efficient use of personnel. The operational procedures of most information systems have the potential to be made more efficient, thereby saving personnel time and increasing productivity. These procedural deficiencies usually surface during the periodic system reviews.

Improved User Interaction

Companies have shown through improved user interaction that productivity in system development can be improved by as much as 400%. The best approach to improving this interaction is to provide an opportunity for users to gain an understanding of MIS principles and the local methods and approaches used to develop and maintain systems. An educational program for MIS professionals should be augmented by ongoing user education programs.

User management and analysts often lack MIS awareness and knowledge (MIS professionals often lack functional area knowledge, also). This affects their ability and desire to cooperate. The old adage "a little education goes a long way" is particularly applicable to MIS education in the user environment.

Development of an in-house user education program will help build lines of communication through a common understanding not only between MIS and users, but between user departments. These user seminars set the stage for more efficient user interaction and increased productivity.

Other approaches to improving user interaction are:

Producing a monthly MIS newsletter.
Involving the user in the systems development methodology.
Establishing a high-level steering committee.
Rotating user personnel to working tours in the MIS department (and vice versa).
Providing a procedure for periodic user feedback relative to MIS performance.

Implementation of a Chargeback System

Only through implementation of a user chargeback system will the user appreciate the scope of their sometimes unnecessary requests for user services. The implementation of a cost allocation and cost control system prompts the user to consider the merit of the request more closely. Much of the systems maintenance done in computer centers without a chargeback system is unnecessary. A request that affects the user's budget causes the user to be more discriminating and to minimize service requests, thereby increasing productivity significantly.

Technology Transfer

A corporate policy encouraging the investigation of the possibility and/or feasibility of technology transfer for software will inevitably yield significant returns by saving personnel time. Rather than "reinvent the wheel" by channeling efforts of programmers and analysts into fundamental application areas, corporations should concentrate on industry-specific application areas for which there is no existing software. The software industry has become very competitive and hundreds of companies offer thousands of products that can save corporate resources.

Exercise

A survey of the personnel at almost any corporation would yield an almost predictable finding. People are most productive in the morning. Invariably, people with sedentary jobs, such as MIS personnel, eat a large lunch, become lethargic, and lose the momentum to work at peak productivity during the afternoon. A simple, yet often scoffed at solution to this problem is midday exercise.

Given the opportunity, many would sacrifice a lengthy lunch and accept a longer working day for the opportunity to engage in midday exercise. Each of twenty professional people surveyed attributed substantial increases in afternoon productivity to their midday exercise routine.

To implement such a program, corporate and/or department policy should be altered to encourage midday exercise and, perhaps, exercise in general. Depending on the relative location of exercise facilities and the type of exercise, an individual may need an extra half-hour at lunch, thereby expanding the working day by the same amount. Policy would be needed to accommodate these instances. The vast majority of those who exercise at midday can complete their exercise routine in less than one hour when shower facilities exist at the work site. Changes in policy and the addition of shower facilities are small corporate concessions for increases in productivity of from 25 to 90% (figures obtained from previously mentioned survey). A conservative cost/benefit analysis would yield a payback period of less than one year (for medium-sized and large corporations) and provide the planner with the flexibility to recommend not only shower facilities, but a comprehensive exercise facility.

Chapter 17

Facilities

The long-range planner should make an assessment of the adequacy of the MIS physical facilities. Common facilities shortcomings are: machine room layout; no controlled distribution center for I/O; laxed security at remote sites; backup data storage facilities in the same building; and MIS professionals scattered throughout a building or several buildings. The planner would be remiss not to address these inadequacies if they exist.

SPACE PLANNING

General Considerations

When computer hardware is scheduled for a particular site, accommodations must be made for power, communications links, and environmental and fire controls. The proliferation of computing hardware has made input from the MIS planner essential in planning for building renovations or for construction of new buildings. Few buildings will escape the need to prepare for some type of hardware installation.

Machine Room

The planner must assess whether more machine rooms are required, more floor space in the central machine room is required, and/or whether the machine room space is effectively utilized. Based on findings, the planner would make the necessary recommendations.

Office Space

Most MIS departments experienced rapid growth in the last ten years. This growth has forced MIS professionals to be spread throughout the corporate offices, often in

155

separate buildings. MIS development requires close coordination and when members of project teams are physically scattered, the quality of the resulting system suffers. The planner will inevitably have to work with corporate and space planners to obtain adequate office space.

The structural reorganization portion of the MIS long-range plan will probably require the planner to reallocate existing or proposed office space such that managers, project teams and/or departments, and so on, are arranged in an optium manner.

Library

Every computer center, no matter how small, should have a library that contains up-to-date DP/MIS books, relevant journals, and specialized materials obtained from seminars, conferences, and informal associations with other corporations. Depending on the accessibility of this library, application systems and program documentation can also be controlled through the library.

Control and Distribution

Ironically, some computer centers realize an enormous volume of input and output, yet there is no room or facility designated specifically for distribution and control of I/O. Not having such a room is an invitation to a security violation.

Conference Rooms

As a rule of thumb, corporations should provide a multiperson conference room for every twenty-five MIS professionals. In many growing data centers, available conference space is reallocated as office space, to the detriment of project team efficiency. The availability of conference rooms promotes the coordination of activities.

Backup Data Storage Facilities

For security reasons, each computer center should have a remote facility in another building in which backup data files are stored. Unfortunately, the importance of such a facility is sometimes realized after the fact; that is, the backup data files are destroyed with the current data files. The planning of such a facility should be at the top of the priority list.

PHYSICAL SECURITY

Data centers handle volumes of sensitive data on a regular basis. For this reason, physical security is critical. The planner should perform some type of risk analysis to assess the level of risk that a corporation is willing to accept. In short, this means how big a padlock you wish to put on the MIS facililties. Unfortunately, some corporations are willing to accept an enormous risk in the hope that no natural or premeditated disaster will occur.

In accomplishing a risk analysis, the planner would assess the adequacy of literally scores of checklist items. For example, the planner might examine the number of access routes to the machine room, whether there is an authorization list for entry into the machine room, the type of fire control system, and so on.

Since security involves virtually every facet of MIS operation, the MIS long-range planner is the logical choice to be assigned the responsibility for security analysis. The following steps constitute a recommended approach for security analysis.

1. *Evaluation of risk*:
   A. Identify and analyze vulnerable areas.
   B. Assign the probability of occurrence of a particular event.
2. *Risk assessment*:
   Establish a level of acceptable risk based on risk evaluation (MIS security is implemented in degrees).
3. *Reduction of risk*:
   Minimize or eliminate threats to vulnerable areas.
   Repeat steps 1, 2, and 3 until the risk is acceptable.

This security analysis should be accomplished in parallel with the MIS long-range plan at least once per year.

Chapter 18

Contingency Planning

The contingency plan is actually a series of plans for each type of occurrence that has the potential to drastically disrupt MIS operation. These occurrences can be a result of individual or group negligence, environmental disaster, or emergency corporate or government requirements. Contingency planning also encompasses planning for other extraordinary occurrences (personnel strike, peacetime to wartime operations for military installations, sudden departure of all key personnel, etc.).

Under normal circumstances, an information services department without a contingency plan can continue to provide adequate service to the corporation indefinitely. However, the department not prepared for other than routine operation is courting corporate disaster. Corporations have gone bankrupt because of the computer center's inability to recover from a disaster and/or provide continuing service to the corporation. Again, the MIS long-range planning function is the catalyst in the preparation of a contingency plan.

APPROACH

Identification of Potential Disasters or Extraordinary Occurrences

The MIS long-range planning committee and the director of MIS should meet with the planner to enumerate potential disasters and extraordinary occurrences to be considered in the contingency plan. The information services department should accept some risk, in that there are marginal returns for developing contingency plans for all possible occurrences. Those disasters and/or occurrences that are most probable and those with the greatest effect on corporate operations should be identified.

Alternate Site Selection

The combined expertise of the MIS long-range planning committee, director, and planner should be used to either select an alternate site(s) for the production function or to ensure that existing facilities are adequate to maintain production systems following a disaster. Existing facilities should be sufficiently secure and/or geographically dispersed to ensure the availability of computer hardware after a disaster or extraordinary occurrence. The recent trend is for corporations to provide their own backup computer capabilities. To do this, some MIS directors have elected two smaller compatible computers rather than one large computer and/or geographic dispersion of equipment.

If an alternate site is selected, the planner should identify conditions under which the alternate site can be used and any necessary hardware/software alterations.

Inevitably, computer time will be limited and production may have to be cut back. The MIS long-range planning committee, director, and planner have the information and expertise to be able to establish relative priorities for production systems. Without established priorities and prior planning, lack of machine time may result in critical activities not being completed.

Contingency Planning Team

A contingency planning team, headed by the MIS long-range planner, should be formulated as a standing team that meets periodically to develop contingency plans and revise those that become out of date. The team typically consists of operational managers in a variety of support areas throughout the corporation. Extremely close coordination is required for MIS contingency planning. When a plan is placed into operation, not only is coordinated support from a variety of corporate support areas critical, but so is timing. The contingency planning team would involve personnel with a direct interest in operations, systems analysis, systems programming, applications programming, internal auditing, legal ramifications, security, data communications, management of MIS, building maintenance, fire protection, transportation, and insurance adjustment. Although the team is made up of corporate employees, input and probably written statements from persons from outside the corporation and/or other companies will be necessary. For example, the legal department should procure and prepare a written reciprocal agreement with cooperating companies and/or vendors.

A contingency planning team would work to provide a contingency plan for each of the areas identified by the MIS long-range planning committee, director, and planner. Each plan should outline the duties and responsibilities of each of the functions listed above as well as those of other companies and appropriate persons not employed by the corporation. The contingency plan should also provide logistical details for the physical move of materials to and from the alternate site, if appropriate.

Training

Periodically, a representative of the contingency planning team should meet with involved personnel to explain the contingency plan and, when possible, drill personnel in the procedures set forth in the contingency plan.

Revisions

Circumstances surrounding potential disasters and/or extraordinary occurrences change. The contingency plan should be reviewed no less than once per year to ensure its viability and appropriateness. The plan found lacking in either should be updated.

Chapter 19

Social Impact and Legal Implications

SOCIAL IMPACT

The assessment of the social impact of the various information systems supported by the company is the responsibility of MIS management. This assessment would be made in cooperation with appropriate functional area managers. The MIS long-range planner, in the process of identification of future MIS projects, should work with management to review existing and proposed application systems and to identify systems with the potential for having an adverse social impact.

The social impact can be internal and/or external. The severity of the impact ranges from employees' short-term displeasure with new procedures to the long-term effect of employees losing their colleagues through computerization. These examples illustrate possible adverse internal social impacts of information systems. If it is known that the implementation and, in some cases, the mere consideration of computerization of a particular application system will have an adverse social impact, the planner should factor this into the MIS long-range planning process. After assessing the social impact of the various information systems, the planner should identify alternative solutions to minimize any adverse impact. In most instances, the planner will work with MIS management and corporate and functional area management personnel to reach a solution.

External social impact references those persons (customers, clients, service, creditors, etc.) who have dealings with the company. A change in a procedure might have a significant impact on the corporate image and, therefore, the profitability of the company. For example, a large, multistate public utility company elected to eliminate the local offices in twelve small towns that they serviced. The residents were then asked to mail payments to a central location. The company did not assess the impact of this change in policy and residents became irate at not having the opportunity to hand carry their payment to the local office, or even to mail their payment to the local office. The net result was that the utility company had to reopen the local offices and completely overhaul the newly installed billing system.

LEGAL IMPLICATIONS

If guidelines do not exist, the long-range planner might suggest the development of guidelines such that applications systems will be within the bounds of any applicable law. At present, many legal questions about computers and information systems are being debated for the first time. There exists a paucity of data by which to evaluate these questions. Actuarial data are almost nonexistent and, therefore, insurance against computer crime and negligence is not only expensive, but of questionable worth.

At present, laws governing the information systems industry are few and those that do exist are subject to interpretation. The Privacy Act of 1974, the Foreign Corrupt Practices Act of 1977, and various state laws on privacy are only the skeleton of what will be adopted in the near future.

Computer-based information systems place the company in many situations in which, if something goes wrong, the company would be liable and subject to suit. For example, a man who was essentially communicating with a computer was continually sent dunning notices for not making payments on an automobile. He had not only made all installment payments, but had completed payment in full. The company's records and procedures were in error, but the company forcibly repossessed the automobile without thoroughly checking their procedures and the legal implications. The man had to sue the company for the return of his bought-and-paid-for automobile. The court ordered the automobile returned and the company to pay him a substantial penalty fee.

For years, functional area and MIS personnel have taken legality of operational systems for granted. The enormous complexity of modern information systems provides ample opportunity for negligence to occur. The planner might make an a priori identification of those aspects of the proposed or existing systems which are vulnerable to either premeditated, illegal MIS activities or negligence. In short, the planner must consider the legal ramifications of information-processing systems.

Privacy

The proliferation of federal and state laws encourages the MIS planner and MIS management to adopt policies that accommodate all federal and state laws. This is particularly true for corporations with interstate computer networks. By adopting the privacy principles embodied in HR 1984 (recently introduced in Congress), MIS management can be reasonably assured that production systems will conform to any applicable laws on privacy, state or federal. The following ten principles regarding the privacy of personal data and information can serve as guidelines to meet present and future legislation on privacy.

1. Permit any person to inspect his or her own file and have copies made at reasonable cost.

2. Permit any person to supplement the information in his or her file.
3. Permit the removal of erroneous or irrelevant information and provide that agencies (organizations) and persons to whom material had been previously transferred be notified of its removal.
4. Prohibit the disclosure of information in the file to individuals in agencies (organizations) other than those who need to examine the file in connection with the performance of their duties.
5. Require the maintenance of a record of all persons inspecting such files and their identity and purpose.
6. Ensure that the information be maintained completely and competently with adequate security safeguards.
7. Require that, when information is collected, the individual be told whether the request is mandatory or voluntary and what penalty or loss of benefit will result from noncompliance.
8. Require that the person involved in handling personal information act under a code of fair information practices, know the security procedures, and be subject to penalties for any breaches.
9. Permit anyone wishing to stop receiving mail because his or her name is on a mailing list to have that right.
10. Prohibit agencies or organizations from requiring individuals to give their social security number for any purpose not related to their social security account or not mandated by federal statute.

Fraud and Negligence

There are two categories of illegal MIS activities. The first is negligence, which is usually a result of poor control of I/O. Negligence results when someone dealing with the company is inconvenienced. The aforementioned case of the repossessed automobile is an example of negligence. The other category is a premeditated or conscious effort to defraud the system. An example of this would be the well publicized Equity Funding case.

Virtually any computer-based system, especially one that deals with money and materials, is vulnerable to fraud and has the potential to place the corporation in a compromising position through negligence. For the most part, acts of fraud and negligence are prosecuted under laws that are not designed for handling computer or information systems-related crimes. Although the potential for either act is ever present, the best assurance against such acts is a good system design and an active program of periodic internal audits. A corporate audit group that is independent of the MIS department and capable of auditing complex MIS systems is not only a vehicle to detect potential loopholes in the system, but to document the validity of the system periodically. The Foreign Corrupt Practices Act has encouraged corporations to establish such an internal auditing group. The act requires corporations to maintain tighter internal controls on accounting procedures. To comply, the MIS auditing group should evaluate system and internal accounting controls, document evaluation, correct disclosed weaknesses, and monitor systems and internal accounting controls to ensure ongoing compliance.

Corporations not having an internal MIS auditing group that complies with the Foreign Corrupt Practices Act are compromising their position of defense in the case of negligence suits. If such a group does not exist, the planner should incorporate the formation of such a group into the organization plan (see Chapter 11).

Chapter 20

MIS Image

The data processing, MIS, or information services department has traditionally been one of the most unpopular organizational entities within the corporation. Since the MIS department services most other operational entities, information services has become not only the workhorse, but the whipping boy of the corporation. It is the rare MIS department that does not have image problems.

Should maintenance of MIS image be included in a long-range plan? The acid test: Is it a project that requires significant MIS resources? Yes, it should be. Since everyone's responsibility is nobody's responsibility, a plan with well-defined tasks and responsibilities is usually needed in order to upgrade the MIS image.

Any organization should maintain good relations with its clients. In the case of the MIS department, the clients are the user departments. Most companies have a public relations office to create and maintain a positive corporate image. Although a similar group within MIS is not a requirement, the function should exist. The MIS long-range plan should present a plan for a concerted effort to improve and maintain a good MIS image.

IMAGE IMPROVEMENT

The planner should work with MIS and, perhaps, corporate management to develop approaches for upgrading the image of corporate information services. Inevitably, the planner is given the responsibility for developing these approaches, since solutions must be integrated with other areas of planning. The following are suggested approaches for image improvement.

Change of Name

The term "data processing" no longer reflects the function of the modern computing center. Production has transcended data processing and now produces information for managerial decision making. A good start in image transformation would be to revise the name to use the term information (versus data) (e.g., information services, management information systems).

User Seminars

The lack of user awareness and knowledge in the area of information systems has been a continual deterrent to a well-ordered MIS environment. The in-house presentation of user management and analysts seminars provides not only an exchange of information and knowledge, but the opportunity for MIS and users to work out misunderstandings and differences.

More Responsive Procedures

Identify internal procedures which can be made more responsive to users. As an example, users should not be made to wait two months for a decision on a single service request.

Organizational Level

The director of corporate information services should be located at the vice-president level. The position should be equal in rank with marketing, production, accounting, and other traditional corporate functions. Until this occurs, MIS image will always be a problem (see Chapter 11).

If the director of MIS currently reports to a vice-president, a major corporate reorganization would be required. Such a suggestion would require the planner to compile extensive documentation (budget, scope of services, trends, etc.) to justify the reorganization. The planner and director of MIS must work closely with the president, executive committee, and high-level steering committee to make this inevitable move a reality.

Overcommitments

MIS managers often agree to any schedule or deadline the user wishes at the onset of a project. An overcommitment renders temporary relief from user pressures but invariably backfires, only to irritate the already unstable MIS image. Solving the overcommitment problem requires better quality control over preparation of project schedules and better understanding by the user of the scope of services requested.

User Liaisons

The existence of a designated user liaison provides a direct contact to anyone outside MIS. The entire department immediately becomes more accessible, and accessibility is directly proportional to the quality of the MIS image.

Improvements to Operations

Make the user aware of a continuing effort to make improvements in the operation of production systems. Then follow up by making improvements, where appropriate, in turnaround time, response time, accuracy, security, data entry, distribution, and so on. The MIS image will surely be enhanced if the user is aware that every effort is being made to resolve the MIS problems.

Presentations on Benefits of the Use of Computers

MIS personnel should make an ongoing effort to provide community and corporate services by lecturing on the benefits of the use of computers and information systems. This service should be made available to labor unions, civic groups, and the various departments within the corporation. Fear of the unknown is still a hurdle to information processing.

Incorporation of the User into the Systems Development Methodology

The user should be directly involved in the development of an application system. The involvement should be encouraged by standardized procedures that assign user management and analyst personnel certain responsibilities, which include input, periodic reviews, and sign-offs. Ongoing user involvement instills a sense of accomplishment and gives the user a feeling that they own the application systems, not MIS (and so it should be).

Creation of a Professional Customer-Client Relationship

MIS management should encourage programmers, analysts, and project leaders to present themselves as unbiased professionals. They should be encouraged to show an equal interest in corporate and MIS well-being. The MIS professional has often been criticized for presenting a know-it-all attitude. MIS personnel should exhibit a willingness to learn from users. In short, systems development should be approached as a 50-50 proposition with MIS and users as partners on a team.

Production of a Quality Product

The bottom line to creating a positive MIS image is producing high-quality information systems and providing responsive support to these systems after implementation.

If image is a problem, the MIS long-range plan should include a package designed to upgrade the MIS image.

Chapter 21

Word Processing and
Office Automation

NEED FOR MIS PLANNING IN THE OFFICE ENVIRONMENT

After the basic application systems are implemented, MIS efforts are often concentrated on systems that affect the blue-collar environment, primarily because of the sheer numbers of persons involved and the repetitive nature of the tasks. However, every year white-collar workers are comprising a greater percentage of the work force; yet, only recently has any emphasis been placed on using the computer to make their immediate working environment more efficient and effective.

Productivity among white-collar workers has not kept up with that of blue-collar workers. Surprisingly, professionals spend from 10 to 75% of their time on clerical tasks. Clerical personnel spend 10 to 50% of their time unnecessarily. Any corporation or office with two or more secretaries can justify installing computing hardware and support software to aid office personnel in their routine activities. The question of need is a foregone conclusion, but the method of addressing this need is less clear. The MIS long-range planner should be instrumental in planning and coordinating the introduction of and/or growth of computer-based office applications.

WHAT IS WORD PROCESSING AND OFFICE AUTOMATION?

The terms "word processing" and "office automation" were coined shortly after it became commercially possible to dedicate small computers to word processing. The scope and meaning of these terms has been a source of confusion to MIS professionals, managers, and clerical personnel. For the purposes of this discussion, office automation is assumed to include the following applications: information transfer via telephone, transaction processing, including storage and retrieval; word processing, to mean text handling; and scheduling of office activities. Note that word processing is a subset of office automation.

Assuming that the scope of office automation as described above is correct, an MIS professional might ask why all of the attention to office automation? In reality, office automation is simply another application for computer-based systems. The terms were coined to sell stand-alone systems, but word processing and office automation are simply extensions of the information services function and should be treated as such by the MIS long-range planner. The only reason this topic is treated in a separate chapter is to highlight the uncoordinated proliferation of dedicated stand-alone minicomputers that support word processing and office automation.

PROBLEMS

MIS managers and professionals, in general, have not recognized the need or importance of such basic applications as word processing. As a result, vendors of inexpensive computing devices designed specifically for word processing have, by default, become advisors to user managers. This is an unhealthy situation for any company. A corporation with less than 150 white-collar workers purchased four word-processing systems from four different vendors. Ironically, the four departments had a considerable overlap in information flow, yet the storage media was totally incompatible among the four devices, not to mention the corporate administrative computers. It is time for MIS management to accept the challenge of office automation. The MIS long-range planner can be a catalyst to this end.

Most word-processing computers are expandable to encompass and accommodate systems more often associated with data-processing or information services. Uncontrolled proliferation of these systems will inevitably delay the realization of an integrated corporate data base.

Quality and technical support are serious problems in word-processing hardware. The ease of development and manufacture of word-processing hardware has prompted scores of companies to enter the marketplace. In this highly competitive environment, marketing representatives tend to overcommit and seldom deliver. Such sales tactics further alienate the users from future computer-based endeavors.

PLANNING CONSIDERATIONS

When planning for office automation, coordination and compatibility should be emphasized. Centralized control is a necessary prerequisite to successful implementation and growth of office automation applications. The following justifications are offered for centralized control and support of office automation, hardware, and applications.

1. Most would argue that proliferation of incompatible word-processing devices

should be curtailed. By default, the MIS department, with its available expertise, should be designated to monitor, control, and assist in the implementation of office automation hardware and applications.

2. Stand-alone units can only add to the problems of redundancy and functional autonomy.
3. The most effective word-processing environment will utilize an integrated corporate data base, supported by the MIS department.
4. Word processing and office automation are part of the information services function.
5. Technical expertise in implementation can be developed by MIS professionals and utilized throughout the corporation.

In order for the MIS department to support office automation applications effectively, the MIS long-range planner should:

1. Suggest revisions to the MIS organizational structure and education programs to accomodate word-processing and office automation.
2. Work toward the adoption of a written corporate policy statement on the purchase and support of office automation hardware and applications (see Chapter 7).
3. Suggest standard procedures for vendor interactions.
4. Suggest standards that will ensure hardware and design compatibility.

The key to successful corporate implementation of word-processing and office automation applications is to automate one office successfully. In no other application is resistance to change more acute. Wholesale implementation of word processing can result in chaos. By far, the best full-scale implementation approach is via a successful pilot project and subsequent demonstration.

The planner has no option but to include office automation in the MIS long-range plan. Years of neglect by many MIS departments has set the stage for uncontrolled proliferation of office automation hardware. Further neglect could slow progress in corporate information services to a standstill.

Chapter 22

Costs

An MIS long-range plan provides sufficient information to make rough estimates of certain project and operational costs. A cost summary will prove helpful in defining budget requirements over the planning horizon; however, a section on costs is not necessarily a required addition to a comprehensive MIS long-range plan. In fact, there is some danger in making cost estimates based on limited information. But as long as the cost summary is recognized as an accumulation of rough estimates for long-range budget planning, a summary of costs can be safely included in the plan.

SUMMARIZING COSTS

For clarity, costs should be summarized within the context of a minimum of cost categories (e.g., labor, travel, etc.). Since a typical MIS project would have project (one-time) costs and the cost of ongoing operations (recurring costs), the costs are further divided into one-time and recurring costs. Figure 22-1 illustrates how one-time and recurring costs can be presented in a minimum of cost categories by project, by budget center, and for the corporation as a whole.

Hierarchy of Cost Summaries

The mere volume of individual cost summaries (by project and budget center and overall) would make extraction of cost data and information difficult without some method to organize the individual cost summaries. The four-level Heirarchy of Cost Summaries shown in Figure 22-2 illustrates how this might be done. Levels A and B present cost summaries without regard to a particular project. Summaries are presented at level A as total costs to the corporation for MIS activities. At level B, total costs are presented by budget centers, primarily the information services department and the various user departments. Levels C and D are cost summaries by project.

Level (1)	Budget Center (levels B and D only) (2)	Project Title and Number (level C and D only) (3)

Cost item		One-time cost	Yearly recurring costs							
		Year (8)	Year 1 (10)	Year 2	Year 3	Year 4	Year 5	Year 6	Year 7	Year 8
Labor										
	(4)									
		(9)					(11)			
Mat. and Eq.	Materials (5)									
	Equipment									
Travel	Per diem (6)									
	Transportation									
Miscellaneous										
	(7)									
Total costs (12)										

Figure 22-1. *Cost Summary.*

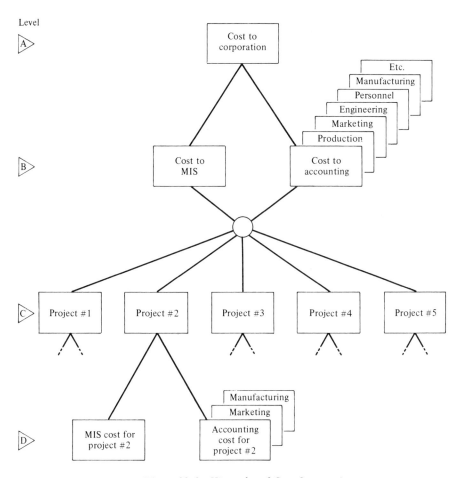

Figure 22-2. Hierarchy of Cost Summaries.

Total cost for a given project is summarized at level C. At level D costs are summarized by project by budget center. Each block represented in the Hierarchy of Cost Summaries represents one completed Cost Summary form. The Cost Summary form is prepared in the same way, but with a different orientation for each level. An individual desiring cost information would first look at the Hierarchy of Cost Summaries as an index for the cost summary desired.

Cost Summary Form

In the Cost Summary form presented in Figure 22-1, the cost categories are:

> Labor
> Materials and equipment

Travel
Miscellaneous

For each category, one-time cost estimates are noted in the first column and recurring cost estimates are noted over the horizon of the MIS long-range plan.

The circled numbers in the item entry locations of Figure 22-1 are cross-references to the following explanations.

1. *Level of cost summary*: cross-reference to the Hierarchy of Cost Summaries.
   A. Summary of all costs to the corporation
   B. Summary of costs to each budget center
   C. Summary of costs for each project
   D. Summary of costs for each project by budget center
2. *Budget center*: applicable to levels B and D only in the Hierarchy of Cost Summaries. Note the applicable budget center (information services, accounting, production, etc.).
3. *Project title and number*: applicable to levels C and D only (Figure 22-2). Each project should be titled and numbered for cross-reference to the Hierarchy of Cost Summaries.
4. *Labor cost*: Break down labor costs by appropriate positions (user management, MIS management, systems analysts, programmers, user clerks, etc.) and list titles in the spaces provided. A titled entry may represent more than one person (e.g., six systems analysts). The level of detail depicted is up to the MIS long-range planner. For any given year, the planner may elect to note the number of person-months involved by including that number in parentheses to the right of the associated cost figure [e.g., $6000 (3)]. The person-month figure is optional.
5. *Materials and equipment cost*: Itemize costs for materials and equipment.
6. *Travel cost*: Itemize costs for per diem and transportation.
7. *Miscellaneous costs*: Any cost item that cannot be classified as labor, materials and equipment, or travel should be listed under miscellaneous (e.g., remodeling machine room to accommodate new equipment).
8. *Beginning year of project*.
9. *Estimated one-time costs*: estimates by cost item of one-time costs for the project. Since no project association exists at levels A and B (Figure 22-2), one-time costs are added to operation costs in the appropriate year.
10. *Year indicators*: In the first column note the first year of the horizon of the MIS long-range plan (e.g., 1983). Label columns to the right accordingly (e.g., 1984, 1985, etc.).
11. *Yearly recurring costs*: Itemize yearly recurring costs for each cost category over the horizon of the MIS long-range plan.
12. *Total cost*: Total project costs are presented as one-time and yearly recurring costs on C and D level summaries. Project costs are combined on A and B

level summaries, with one-time costs noted in the year they are expected to be incurred. Fluctuations in the dollar make adjustment for inflation, and consequently a discounted total dollar figure, difficult to compute. Yearly estimates are more valuable than a discounted total cost figure.

The Cost Summary is prepared at level D by the budget center for each project. These cost items are accumulated and presented on a single form for each project at level C. Level B Cost Summaries are prepared by accumulating all costs for each budget center Cost Summary at level D. The single corporate Cost Summary form at level A is prepared by accumulating all Cost Summaries at level B.

Some Cost Summaries may require explanations to clarify certain entries. This is accomplished by simply attaching the details and an explanation to the appropriate Cost Summary.

Appendix

Case Studies

A prerequisite to successful MIS long-range planning is a planning methodology. The methodology will invariably exhibit the personal touch of the developer
and accommodate the idiosyncrasies of the corporation; therefore, the planning
process will be approached in many different ways. This appendix presents two brief
case studies of how a medium-sized (MED) and a large (BIG) organization
approached their initial MIS long-range planning effort.

MED CORPORATION

MED (a fictitious name) is a company of over 18,000 employees headquartered in the
southwestern part of the United States. Although 70% of the employees work at the
headquarters location, others are spread geographically over the world. The primary
product is oil. At the beginning of the planning process, they had a single large-scale
IBM processor with a number of remote minicomputers and peripherals from a
variety of manufacturers. The central computing facility (MIS Department) has over
300 employees; two-thirds are considered professional. MED had no existing MIS
long-range plan.

 Top-level management designated a senior systems analyst, a former project
team leader, to be the MIS Long-Range Planner. This person had been employed in
the MIS Department for ten years and had a broad range of experience with the
various application systems and user departments.

 A staff position called "Long-Range Planner" was created. This position reported to the Director of MIS, a vice-president of the company.

 The planner was given the latitude and flexibility to determine the method for
developing the plan and the actual format and contents of the plan. Both the process
and the end product were subject to ratification by the Director of MIS.

 The Long-Range Planner established the Planning Committee, made up of key

managers within the MIS Department. The committee was not established to develop the plan, but to serve as a vehicle to provide feedback from the various facets of
the MIS Department.

The MED planner had no experience in MIS long-range planning, nor did
anyone else at MED. The first three months on the job were spent primarily in
examining written material on planning and in discussions with those who have had
experience in MIS planning. Informally, the planner talked with his colleagues to obtain their perception of how to proceed and on the scope of the MIS long-range plan.

Having studied alternative approaches to the planning process, the planner
developed a methodology for accomplishing the MIS long-range plan. The methodology and approach had many similarities to that described in this book. The
Planning Committee was an integral part of the methodology.

The Planning Committee, chaired by the planner, met periodically to approve or
disapprove ideas developed and presented by the Long-Range Planner (these ideas
could have been submitted to the planner by persons within MIS or from users). The
committee meetings served the function set forth by the planner. However, emotions
were always high on almost any given topic. Initially, the chairman had a very
difficult time maintaining adherence to an agenda. As an example, when strategic
planning was the objective, discussions often degenerated to such topics as the
number of programmers per interactive terminal.

All preliminary sessions of the Planning Committee were devoted entirely to
strategic planning. The chairman charged the committee with establishing goals and
objectives for each major functional area within the MIS Department. The goals and
objectives were established after numerous meetings and three months' elapsed
time. After the MIS goals and objectives were determined, the process continued in a
hierarchical manner, with each major objective area being subdivided into more
manageable levels. The detailed plan was completed one year after the goals and
objectives were established.

The MED methodology did not accommodate user input directly. A major
premise of the long-range planning methodology was that functional area managers
within the MIS department had sufficient contact with the user to be able to obtain
feedback and pass it on to members of the Planning Committee. After completing
the long-range plan, committee members felt this to be a valid premise. (Later it was
apparent that the lack of direct user interaction with the Long-Range Planner was a
mistake to be rectified in future MIS long-range plans.)

MED's policy is to update the MIS long-range plan once per year. They
estimate nine person-months of effort to accomplish this task. This is essentially one
person full-time the year around. MED is now engaged in a continuous effort in MIS
long-range planning.

BIG FEDERAL AGENCY

BIG (a fictitious name) is a federal agency with "data-processing" installations in over
200 locations throughout the United States and the world. Over 5000 personnel are

directly associated with the data-processing (DP) function, with 1000 at Headquarters DP. The nerve center of BIG's DP operation is, like most federal agencies, located in Washington, D.C. Headquarters DP provides standardized software, direction, and guidance to the satellite installations, but does not have line authority.

Although BIG has engaged in some planning efforts, the initiation of a comprehensive and ongoing planning effort was hampered by rapid turnover in top DP management. The net effect of management's inability to coordinate the DP activities of the many subdivisions of BIG was virtually no forward progress. At best, BIG was maintaining the status quo with respect to DP. To keep abreast of state-of-the-art DP and computer technology, BIG's DP management determined that their only option was to complete a "Master Plan," what amounted to a comprehensive long-range plan for data processing.

Although a headquarters planning group existed, the group functioned primarily to assist various DP areas and satellite installations in short-term planning. The group had no charge nor the necessary internal clout to address the topic of integrated planning.

The scope of the proposed Master Plan was too encompassing to be accomplished directly by top DP management. However, the scope of the planning effort required the knowledge of seasoned high-level managers; thus, a Master Planning Group was established.

Under most circumstances, staffing of a new group would not be a serious problem; however, the demands of the Master Planning Group required senior-level personnel with a broad knowledge of BIG's operation. The most obvious choices were managers of several of the largest operational DP units. Each person selected was very successful at his or her present position and would be hard to replace, but the fact remained that to create a viable Master Plan, these people were needed. Certainly, there was a trade-off between taking valuable managers from their management positions and asking them to dedicate two years to a planning effort. The Master Plan was of such importance to the ultimate success of BIG's DP function and BIG in general that the sacrifice was made. The Master Planning Group was established as a staff function that reported to the director. The initial complement was six high-level DP professionals plus two support personnel. Three of the six professionals came from high-level line management positions (reported to Director of DP).

To provide continuity within the Master Planning Group, a schedule of rotation was established such that these high-level managers could rotate back to commensurate or higher-level positions after two or three years on the Master Planning Group. The rotations were time-phased such that a nucleus always existed.

The Master Planning Group, which was given a free hand to move throughout DP and BIG, was given the following charges:

Concentrate on the overall BIG objective.
Develop a Master Plan within the scope of DP responsibility.

Recommend DP long-range planning interest areas and priorities to the Director of DP.

Establish planning guidelines for more detailed planning to be accomplished at lower levels and oversee the diverse DP planning efforts throughout BIG.

Compile and maintain an overall Master Plan and coordinate the detailed subordinate plans.

It was anticipated that ultimately the Master Planning Group would have a network of planners throughout BIG. These planner would be attracted to their functional units and coordinate all planning activities through the Master Planning Group.

To complement the Master Planning Group, a committee of outside experts was assembled. This group of experts is called the Planning Assistance Committee and has an ongoing membership of from four to seven DP specialists from separate governmental, industrial, and/or educational organizations. Each represents a specific area of DP endeavor (management, communications, systems software, etc.).

The primary function of the Planning Assistance Committee is to provide feedback on alternatives proposed by the Master Planning Group and to offer different perspectives on suggested approaches, or perhaps suggest approaches themselves. The Planning Assistance Committee convenes monthly to review approaches to solutions suggested by the Master Planning Group.

The Planning Assistance Committee has no power to veto ideas or approaches. Their vehicle for expressing concern over a proposed approach is first to discuss their ideas with the Master Planning Group. When neither persuades the other, the Planning Assistance Committee sends a "statement of difference," with justification, to the Director of DP. Like the Master Planning Group, appointments to the Planning Assistance Committee are limited to two years to minimize the possibility of members becoming stagnant.

The third of three major groups involved in BIG's approach to DP planning is the User Steering Committee. The User Steering Committee consists of high-level user managers throughout BIG. This committee is charged with providing feedback on system development project priorities and with arbitrating differences that relate to DP.

Since this was the initial DP planning effort, top DP management defined the scope of the effort. The initial plan addressed general areas, not specific DP operational deficiencies. Shortcomings and deficiencies are addressed in lower-level detailed plans that are coordinated by the Master Plan. The Master Plan identified the general content, approach, and guidelines for the development of the various subordinate plans.

The Master Plan was originally prepared without regard to current operations or government restrictions. The premise of this approach was that, after assessing the feasibility of the ideal, the plan could be tempered to a compromise between the ideal and that which is practical.

It was recognized that a tremendous amount of overlap in the planning areas existed, but to make the planning task more intelligible, the Master Planning Group identified sixteen planning areas. Each planning area had several major subdivisions. This logical segmentation provided at least a starting point and some meaningful structure to the planning effort.

The Master Planning Group, the Planning Assistance Committee, the User Steering Committee, and the Director of DP form the framework for what one person described as a "terrifyingly complex, but do-able Master Plan."

Index